OTHER BOOKS BY FRANK LIMA

Inventory, Tibor de Nagy Gallery (1964)
Underground with the Oriole, E.P. Dutton (1971)
Angel, W.W. Norton/Liveright (1976)

INVENTORY

INVENTORY

New & Selected Poems

Frank Lima

Edited by David Shapiro

HARD PRESS, INC. 1997

Many thanks to the editors of *Evergreen Review, The Paris Review, Wagner College Review, C Magazine, Poetry, The Little Magazine, Unmuzzled Ox, Boss 5, Confrontation, Mother, Roof II, Broadway, Shell, Adventures in Poetry, Nuestro, The Ant's Forefoot #11, The World, lingo: A Journal of the Arts, Cover,* and *The American Poetry Review,* where some of these poems were first published.

Cover painting of Frank Lima by Elaine de Kooning,
courtesy of Mrs. M. Luyckz
Typeset in 10.5 New Baskerville by Chad Odefey

Published in the United States by
Hard Press, Inc.,
a non-profit organization:
PO Box 184
West Stockbridge, MA 01266
ISBN 1-889097-10-1

Lima, Frank, 1939-
Inventory, new and selected poems / Frank Lima.
p. cm. – (Profile series)
ISBN 1-889097-10-1 (alk. paper)
I. Title II. Series: Profile series (Hard Press)
PS3562.I46I58 1997
811'.54–dc21 97-8776
CIP

to my wife
Helen

CONTENTS

IV. From *ANGEL*

V. From *YEAR'S END*

VI. From *TULUM*

VII. From *ORFEO*

FRANK LIMA: The Poetry of Everyday Life and the Tradition of American Darkness

To Elaine de Kooning

Frank Lima's poetry is a poetry of everyday life, but only a poet of enormous strength and fearlessness is capable of describing the everyday. One might say that the life Lima describes is so exceptional that it cannot or should not be placed under the idea of the everyday. But I think his inventory of traumata in childhood, of drugs and dangers, of incarceration and release, of his triumphs as a man, a father and husband, a cook, a translator, an artist—this inventory in its inclusiveness of urban space is exactly what the French thinker Lefebre meant by the production of the everyday. Lefebre suggested that the real philosophy of modern life could be accomplished by the description of a single day. Lima, learning from poets as various as Villon, Neruda, O'Hara, Lowell, and Corbière, emerges with a mixture of day and dream that is a maximal realism and rendering of his more than half-century of living. It's a story of survival and, crowned by his compassion, much more than any facile listing of a victim's horrors. He concludes this volume with extraordinary poems of religious depth and poems that create a public, even vatic voice—poems for all victims, for a Hasidic youth, for those bombed in Oklahoma, for an older mortal prophet, and for his own children glimpsed in their fragility and resilience.

This development towards poems of wisdom is an unexpected delight and a sign of his status as a major poet. When I met him in 1962 Frank Lima had already written extraordinarily sensuous descriptions of the street and the body, and he had already conquered any timidity in poems that shocked everyone concerning incest, drugs and violence. Instead of pursuing this as a single reductive mode, Lima accepted influences and worlds that made him larger and richer. He showed a disdain, he once told me, for Beat poets who wanted to return to a poverty he wanted to transcend. He was always willing to look backwards and even with nostalgia he studied, but he had a ferocious way of engulfing new experiences. After the first volume, and early poems that are as poignantly particular and sharp as prison slang, he learned from Frank O'Hara and wrote poems that sweep us into abstractions and stories that are mythical and urbane and humorous. He had always had this humor, as in his eerie comparison of a lover to a judge of the criminal courts, but the poems now accepted and assimilated a disjunctive poetics of the New York School. He loved this tough art of welding disparate poetic worlds, and dedicated his own art to that of David Smith's heraldic and monumental sculpture.

He has never stopped learning, never stopped being a student of himself, language, and the city. He became a master chef, cooking having always been one of his talents, received a master's degree from Columbia with the same earnestness that had led him to study Villon in his teen years even while in rehabilitation, and he has now become the master of a magical-realist style that I identify with Marquez as much as Neruda. Strangely, he has turned a prose fragment into a dazzling lyrical-narrative autobiographical sequence. In the future, we may expect more from this novelistic mode that includes amazing cinematic sequences, for example, a horrifying scene in which he observes his father drunk and near death in a park. Lima, a New York Surrealist, completely seizes the rage and detachment and strangeness of this vision. It is something he accomplishes from his earliest work, but now it is not just snapshot photography at its best—no small achievement itself—but a masque-like architecture of great scale, where the instants add up to a whole social vision.

After our first amazing meeting, I was touched by what Kenneth Koch called, in his introduction to the first chapbook of his poems, his courage and his honesty about pleasure and poverty. These early poems are still luminous achievements, and there can be no anthology of the last fifty years of poetry that does not include something of these amazing poems without a loss. No poem that I know of speaks like "Mom I'm All Screwed Up" about childhood torments and its ferocious intimacies. No city poems about Spanish Harlem have ever yielded the completely convincing tones of these early works. They are fast, furious, and alive with the musical grace found in this sudden bit of landscape and church music from "Abuela's Wake":

"Dios te salve Maria
Dios te salve Maria
outside
the snow-mouth of December tinked on the windows"

"Pudgy" rises to the sweetest and most serious sensuality in "O my chocolate princess / I lay in bed / smelling of Lifebuoy soap and toothpaste / light a stogie and watch the smoke / unshoe ghost-nude thoughts." This is a poetry of a young man with great insight into the body's possibilities, but it is important to realize that he didn't stop with this kind of expressiveness.

He went to school with the "ordinariness" of the New York School and the empiricism of his great friend and mentor, Frank O'Hara, and always learned too from the perfected finesse of Kenneth Koch. With such a different vision, it is hard to believe that he could synthesize these elements, to subulate them into his turbulent scenes: "where the fish bring light to the sun / waiting for the weakness of a dreamer." But that is exactly the task of his middle-period lyrics and prose in which he mixes hedonism, picturesque whimsy, and his particular form of honesty, emerging with extraordinary strange tales of the ordinary as in his "1/2 Sonnet," or his suddenly violent "Plena" or "Postcard" or "Patchouli." If his usual forte and dramatic instrument was naturalist description, he had now expanded his palette to include something as large and "anthropologically" vast as his "Cuauhtemoc": "I always bring captives here / and let the grapevine choke them."

The snapshot aesthetic of Robert Frank is thus given a funny and more intense inflection when it collides with the possibilities of a kind of historical or historicized surrealism. The search for the marvelous should not be mere and should not cut poetry off from its worldliness: "The face of poetry is an expressive cut of meat that gives us a glimpse of truth." Lima has a tremendous, almost compulsive need for truth-telling, and one remembers that Paul Goodman once suggested that poets did not write novels, not because of a lack of imagination, but because they had a compulsion to avoid fiction in a love of wild truth. This is why Lima's New York School use of symbolism and surrealism never led him away from his solid sense of thing and fact, boundless body and private street. If anything, he reminds us that the Surrealists at their best—one thinks of the Aragon that Benjamin loved in *Paysan de Paris*—were a final if seemingly superstitious stroke of realism in its extremity. Lima's works, like Schwitters' Merz constructions—are towers of the convoluted debris of everyday life and not reduced ejaculations or cries of protest. This is what Koch admired early in their lack of moralism, and it is to his credit that even in this sense, Lima has been able to develop, so that strangely his new moral-religious odes are willing to add to his snapshots of the marvellous in the everyday a new cognitive dimension. His integrity in developing this moral dimension might be said to occur in poems in which he is more parent than son, more citizen than nomad.

Thus, I find Lima's journey from the poems of prison, drug-addiction and the frenzy of sexuality to his new poems and autobiographical narratives to be a triumph of what Erik Ericson used to speak of as the antinomy of wisdom and bitterness. In these poems, again and again, his early toughness is matched by a gentle largeness of generosity and something elegiac that seems necessary and not politically pretentious. He can write about the "shadow of the twentieth century" because he feels it, in Keatsian negative capability, "on my liver," and thus his ode to the Cedar Bar poets is as personal as the most personist of O'Hara. I think any critic will want to praise the imaginative vividness, syncretism and "publicness" of these new orchestral poems. It is enough to tell the truth, though O'Hara used to joke that that was all that was necessary and form was as simple as a good fit in clothes, but the truth slant as in Dickinson is the proper opaque for a master like Lima of what I have called the tradition of American darkness.

I have always admired Lima's Whitmanesque wit and wisdom, and I recall that he once laughed back at an older poet who had told students at Columbia that they needed more solitude, "I've been in solitary and I don't need more solitude." I like his human and humorous poems, and in his late poems, like "Father's Day," he creates his own apotheosis and dissemination: "I have seen the seeds in our seeds / Become an army of paper children ... An imperfect father gives his / Children a drawing of an old Sun." He can be as gently attenuated as a Valery Larbaud in his food poems ("Ode to Julia Child"), but these are just his most recent scherzi. The new magnitude in his work is seen in his homage to a ancient Mexico and to the tenderness of poets: "Allen will be taken from us / to the slaughterhouse of dear God." Somehow I trust his Jewish and his Catholic poems, his poems of an unbearable ethnicity, and his poems of a soaring universalism. Isaiah Berlin has taught us to dream less and less of an homogenized world of unconflicted happiness. Lima is a tragic pluralist, who knows what it's like to be almost run over in social collisions. He has gone from a poem as subtle and slangy as "In Memory of Eugene Perez" to a poem as sustained and furious as his "Oklahoma America." I have always enjoyed the way Frank Lima disdained poets who too greedily used their origins to gain a false publicity. He has an amazing lack of self-pity, both in his poems and in his presentation of himself, but I do pity those who neglect his voice and wise rage at their peril. I think Lima's story and his fabulous dark insistence are one of the most remarkable American triumphs. We have witnessed, in these thirty-five years, along with his friend, that amazing cubo-futurist Joe Ceravolo, the creation of a mature American poetry of everyday darkness.

Frank Lima could have stopped when he had finished his Rimbaudien poems of the street, rough and physical and full of caricature. He could have also accepted complacently his re-formulation of the New York School and stopped as a poet with a control of surrealism and urbane fancy. He has refused to stop, and his poetry today has the rare public-private synthesis that counts, and a supernatural naturalism that underlines him, in M.H. Abrams's sense, as a late Romantic. He finds in the turbulent darkness of New York and America his mythology, his Alps, his truth.

David Shapiro
New York City, 1996

Note:

We owe a debt of gratitude to the painter, Sherman Drexler, who gave the teen-aged Lima books of François Villon, Robert Lowell, and French symbolist poetry and told him to write the way he spoke. Think of the good sense of that magnanimous advice and the intrepidity with which Lima repaid his friend, to whom he dedicated the first of his books, like this entitled *Inventory*. Drexler remembers telling Lima that nothing could embarrass him, and the unembarrassed courage of this poetry has been the startling result and theme and commitment of this poet of particulars.

Editing this volume of inventories has largely been the author's work, and I have collaborated and intervened mostly to encourage and mediate his own true sense of his poetry. Both of us have had to realize there is enough left out to make another volume of past work and at least another of recent lyrics. I was lucky to be the first recipient of many of these poems, and I am still digesting the good fortune of watching them occur. The selection is partial, but it prides itself on being a fair perspective on the daily richness of an artist who continues to make his complete works even larger and more surprising.

I. SCATTERED VIGNETTES

SCATTERED VIGNETTES

I remember what I remember
I remember writing a poem
About me
About you
About the Christ
About the thing in the garden:

We were stars in my mother's belly.
We were the faces of the angels;
like the angels we came into this world
with blood on our wings.

The angels are God's hit squad:
Whenever He wanted someone assassinated,
He sent an angel to do His dirty work:
Sodom and Gomorrah.
The angels always smell
like fine cigars.

My father's mother was a poor Indian who made
and sold confections in the streets
of Guadalajara to make ends meet.
The town doctor was
Don Francisco Lima,
of Castilian descent
and my grandmother,
Benigna's, paramour.

Don Francisco died when my father was very young.
My grandmother
armed herself with a gun
and took my father to the
funeral to see his father for the last time.

This was scandalous to
Don Francisco's grieving family,
and his practice which was the entire town.

As a boy I imagined my grandmother
stepping out of a Paul Muni cloud of dust
with a long barreled gun in one hand
and this filthy neonate in tow in the other hand.

The white European-descent-small-Mexican-town aristocracy
must have shit in their white stucco catholic church!

My father would relate these events to me
while at the kitchen table,
in tears,
between drinks on his only day off.
When my father spoke of his childhood
in Mexico,
I could hear the mariachis singing
"La Paloma" in the background
and see the white dove on the windowsill.

One hot, dry day after the funeral my grandmother,
accompanied by my father, was selling her candies
when she was approached by a young man on horseback
who turned out to be my father's half brother.

He was abusive to my father's mother.
Why else
would one hack his own half brother to death?

My father fled the country.
He was wanted for murder.
The story got murky.
My father was drunk and pissing in his pants.

I don't remember him ever vomiting;
he was a real pro.

Anyway,
he became a romantic fugitive
bumming around the country eating raw potatoes,
iguanas (the Mexican walking lunch)
and hiding in abandoned barns and farm houses.

He finally made his way east to Veracruz
where he boarded a merchant ship bound for Europe.
He was a stowaway.

His tale of survival was permeated with spirits
and machismo.
He hid in a coal bin
and ate whatever moved within his reach.
He was discovered by a stoker
who took pity on his emaciated
and filthy condition.
This chthonic creature
from the bowels of the ship
saved my father's life
by sharing stale bread
and rotten vegetables with him.

My father was convinced
the stoker
was not what he appeared to be.
He was the *vision serpent* sent
by his forefathers to rescue him:

> the stoker's aspect would change
> from a man to an animal:
> sometimes he appeared before my
> father as a bat with bread
> as a snake with water or
> when my father was homesick
> and missed his mother
> the stoker would appear
> as a spider with sugar

My father was not afraid of the dark.
It was its vastness
and lack of sunlight
that my father found foreboding and ominous.

In the immensity of that metal darkness
he would cry for the sun to appear
and blind his mind of all memory:

his tears were
tiny glass scorpions
tumbling from his face,
shattering on the floor
forming little pools
of light

The soot-covered wingless angel
of mercy never betrayed my father's
whereabouts to anyone onboard ship.
My father expressed these events
to me
with reverence
as if he were reciting
a long forgotten prayer.
Although he was frozen and silent,
I imagined his eyes
were speaking to me
and divulging secret adventures
that I would
understand when I got older.
Perhaps even undertake myself.

My father never spoke to me
or my brothers while he was sober.
He was proud of the scars on his face
and a bullet embedded in his back
that looked like a baby trying to escape
from a flaccid marshmallow Easter egg.

He never played with us or touched us
except when he was drunk.
On Sunday mornings he would wake us up:
He would be wearing my mother's negligee,
her bra, exaggerated makeup and sloppy lipstick.

He would come into our beds to roughhouse with us.
Through my mother's nightgown I could see
and feel the hair on his body,
like chicken wire covered with velvet.

On Sunday mornings I attended mass at Saint Cecilia's
Roman Catholic church with my grandmother,
Dolores, which is plural for pain: Many pains.
She was my mother's mother.

I was an altar boy
in the service of the church
and the almighty Father Archangel
who perspired a lot no matter what the weather was.
A pious man whose gullet
was the ciborium of the
sacred blood of Christ:
Each day,
at dusk,
Father Archangel was in a
sublunary alcoholic fog,
stumbling and grunting in the sacristy,
shooing away the floating angels
he had disgorged into the piscina.

He was often hungover and irritable
the following day and acted as if
he had survived a meaningless war
where he had lost every thing,
his biretta,
his immortal soul.

He would be out of spiritual breath
as he climbed out of his wine-colored pit.
During these humane interludes,
he would often speak to me
in quiet tones about the priesthood
and its burdens.

One such burden was his erotic dreams
and the torments he suffered
when he had an erection.
He would ask me if I,
at my age,
had erotic dreams and erections.
He would never let me answer the questions,

and interject, reassuringly,
that it was natural and physical.

I knew at that instance he had another
ecclesiastical attack of libidinal repentance.
What is the act of contrition
for a twelve year old priest-fucker?

I thought,
how can I get kicked out of the mother church?
Get excommunicated!
In those days there was no such thing
as ratting-out an aging,
fag priest.

It came to me in a walking dream
on my way home from school:
Saturday night when everyone was asleep
I took my mother's Alka-Seltzer
from the medicine cabinet,
unwrapped them carefully
and placed them in a napkin in my
Sunday-pants' pocket.
Sunday morning before mass
I very carefully substituted
the holy wafers with the Alka-Seltzer.
I arranged them in such a way
that every other person would receive
one Alka-Seltzer.

I felt an extraordinary feeling of accomplishment
and genius for someone who could not read the word "the."
At the same time I was petrified with fear;
my legs were weak and would not carry me.
It was going to be the end of the world.

The Daily News would carry the story
when the smoked cleared
and they found my beige body.

That was wishful thinking.
The big white finger in the sky
would get me first and drill me
like a gimlet right into hell!

Maybe I could cut a deal with the devil and paint signs for him.
It was the only thing I did well in school.
Maybe I could learn to read in hell.
Anyway, I would get there before Father Archangel
and whack him since I was already in hell.

The eucharistic rite was in slow motion:
Father Archangel was shining and white,
floating in the air as he performed the rites.
My feeling was he knew what was going to happen
and deliberately let it happen in order to become
a martyr and a saint.

There were millions of expectant parishioners
in the church that morning.
Saint Cecilias,
a church no bigger than a house fly,
in the village of Spanish Harlem,
had miraculously become a gigantic cathedral that morning
because it knew that an extraordinary event would take place
and that I was responsible.

Then everything stopped moving
except for Archangel's hands
inserting the holy wafer
into the open mouths of the expectant parishioners
that instantly erupted belching white foamy lava.

They were like mad dogs foaming at the mouth
and barking at the oblivious priest
as he held the apocryphal Grail up to heaven
offering my beige body,
my blood
to Jesus Christ.
He screamed!

And I disappeared
into a long puff
of marijuana,
alcohol and drugs.

My mother is a *Santera*:
Santerismo is not witchcraft.
Witchcraft implies evil doing.
In Santerismo
the person who offers the service
is the belief system.
The services can bring harm to someone;
can right a wrong;
effect a cure of an illness;
attract or drive away a lover.

She employs auguries,
strange forms of phylacteries,
talismans
and all manner of potions,
including rituals for unrequited love when
menstrua occurs.

Notwithstanding,
a *Santera* is a medium,
a vessel for the spirits from heaven or hell:
These spirits would occupy my mother's body
and use her faculties to communicate with the payee.
She did well.

The procurer of my mother's services would benefit,
therefore it is not considered evil.

Only the two demons that are at the right and left
of the devil, *Altaro, Altaclan,* and the one in front of him,
the most malefic, *Altaru,* are evil.
Therefore, one respects the devil
as he directly does not cause evil.
Evil is the invocation and not the act of placing a glass
of clear water with a rose in it on a windowsill.

My mother would dress me up
in little girls' dresses
before I was old
enough to attend school.

She often photographed me on these occasions
and would show them to her friends with the
casualness of a reminiscing parent.
And with the manners of a pedantic official,
she would speak of me as if I were far away
attending some wonderful college.

In this *tableau vivant*,
my mother would mention that she always wanted a girl.
In these soft black and white photographs
I would be wearing a voluminous
white dress;
bobby socks
and buckled shoes to match;
my hair was long and curly,
and arranged in a coif of light colored ribbons.
I had a puzzled look on my face.

When I began grade school I was ashamed
to go to the boys' room with the other boys
because I was wearing little girl's underwear that were
pink and shiny.

While my father was at work,
my mother had male friends visit her.
I was forbidden to ever mention these visits to my father
or my grandparents who lived in the same building just
across the hall:

My family and my mother's family occupied the entire floor.
We were told (I have two younger brothers, Phillip and Kelly)
to stay in our room during these visitations.
I would sneak out and watch my mother engage
in acts with these men that I had witnessed the
night before while my mother and father thought
we were asleep.

I remember one of my mother's paramours in particular,
el Patilludo, the one with exaggerated sideburns.
He was always attired in black bell bottom pants and had shiny,
black mummified hair that was as sleek and tight as a shower cap
on his head and obviously attended to with laborious care.
He was taller than my mother.
I would watch: He would be kneeling in front of her
between her legs in the kitchen as that was the farthest room
and the most remote from the bedroom.

He would have tears in his eyes that accumulated
on his mustache like icicles.
My mother would lovingly,
with the tip of her tongue,
lick the tears from his eyes.

El Patilludo looked like one of the flamenco dancers
in a poster that hung in the living room.

I once overheard my mother mention that he reminded
her of Valentino, the great lover of silent films.
Yeah, right. Only if Valentino had the puffy cheeks
of a beer drinker.

My mother's lovers all had code names
as they were more often than not
the surreptitious exchange between her
and her band of house-coat-and-pin-curler friends
immediately following the departure
of one of my mother's lovers.

They were
hungry lionesses
quickly approaching
a freshly killed corpse
of gossip.

My mother was the queen bee who provided
lascivious pollen to these pedestrian drones.

The kitchen was suddenly aglow with
their shiny cold cream faces
and the hushed tones of erotic whispers;
a forum for explicit comparisons of amatory techniques
and erogenous wishful thinking as these women
were all married and would not dare cheat
on their Carlos and Fernando:
Mr. Spanish Dick, Sr.
The consequences would be
facial disfigurement
with a straight razor
or two slashes across the ass,
so she could not lay on her back
and fuck anybody else,
by a self-righteous,
jealous husband who had been
fucking anything that walked,
in the name of his manly,
macho duty because all mighty
God had given him
His only begotten twelve inch dick!

My family life came to an abrupt end
when I mentioned these events to my
grandmother who confronted my mother.
My mother became a beige tropical tower
scintillating anger who threw me out
of the house naked into the hall of
the building for betraying her.
I lived with my grandparents after that.
My mother did not speak to me for months.

At my grandparents',
I listened to the radio late into the night.
The radio was a miniature church with a green,
luminous Christ that emanated music and white,
masculine voices that told stories.

As I listened
late at night,
I ate salt from my left hand,

while turning the dial
with my right hand.
I was the only human being
alive
on the face of the earth
and I was communicating
with fantastic beings
in the green cathode night.

Eventually I returned home. My father was losing
one job after another because of his drinking.
He was hallucinating, chasing away the *vision serpent*
and becoming violent and dangerous.
When my parents separated I remember going to school
on an abandoned iceberg, not being able to read or spell
words that I could the day before for the teacher.
I wrote plays for a puppet theater I had constructed
and recited poetry from memory. All that vanished
when my father left home. Until now that has been
the most tragic event in my life.
The end came one Sunday spring afternoon
at dinner, when, what seemed, without provocation,
my father cut the left side of my mother's face.
In slow motion my brother Phillip and I beat him
with baseball bats into a pool of blood.
I had a .22 caliber automatic Italian Bareta
that I jammed in his face, cocked the trigger,
and told him to back off, to leave.

He looked at me as if he were going to tell me one last
story with his eyes once again, he smiled ever so slightly
and told my mother, without ever taking his Maya-black
eyes from me, that I would cause her the most pain and
trouble. He left and so did the Mariachis and *La Paloma*
on the windowsill.

One summer afternoon some of my boyhood friends told me
that their parents had seen my father on a bench on East
110th in Central Park drinking with a bunch of bums.
I don't remember walking or running to the park to see my
father. I just appeared across the street and he was there,
dirty and unshaven.

He was sitting on a bench with his arms around a woman
who was fat and as dirty as he was. There were other
derelicts on the park bench, but the woman fascinated
me for some unknown reason. Her stockings were loosely
rolled around her ankles. My father's once jet black
hair was grey and as long as the Indians' on TV.
Although it was summer he was wearing a tattered winter
coat that was many sizes too big.

He was Moses-Charlston Heston holding a pint of wine
up to the sky in one hand and the woman's hand in the other.
The bottle was the law and she was his staff.

The woman and my father were both drinking from the same
bottle as if they were sharing some spiritual part of
their lives, some mysterious part of their bodies, with
each other. There was something magical in that bottle
that bound them together. That woman and what was left of
my father would part the sea in my life forever.
I stared and did not cross the street to speak to him.
I vanished as quickly as I appeared into another puff of smoke.

I remember it was a noisy spring in Spanish Harlem when
I came home one evening after running the streets. I found
my mother in the bedroom sitting in front of her Renaissance
Bronx-Italian vanity; her face was glowing with mascara
and rouge. She was wearing large ornamental, miniature
playground-swing earrings made of gold, and all her
jewelry and her favorite perfume, FOLLOW ME: It was a
dark blue bottle with a white decal of a palm tree and
a quarter moon.

Her hair was in what she called her Joan Crawford upsweep,
held in place, in the center, by a large Spanish comb that
was flanked by two long ornate, lethal skewers.

Her eyes were puffy and moist. She looked like a
Chinese emperor with lollipops in her hair. She calmly
faced me and informed me that my father was dead.
Before I uttered a word, she became quite erect and
announced, with an air of glutinous authority,
that the cause of his death was "acute alcoholism."

She almost smiled as if the term would somehow
dignify his condition in Central Park.
As if he were a great casualty of an honorable war.

The fierce caveman in drag was dead.
The warrior who vanquished cirrhotic spirits was dead.

My mother began to drink a lot.
One summer night she was drinking and became ill.
She was glistening with perspiration,
cheap perfume and wrapped in cigarette smoke.
She asked me to help her to bed.

She was wearing a house dress with nothing underneath.
This was shortly after my father's death.
I may have been twelve,
perhaps younger.

She asked me to lie next to her.
I did and fell asleep next to her
with extraordinary anticipation.

When I awoke she was a warm mist hovering,
suspended over me,
naked,
a giant night bird
whose soft long feathers
were sweeping my body away
into the cumulus clouds
of black pubic hair.
My pants were down to my knees.
I looked at her for an instant.
A nano second in a boy's erotic time.

She was startled.
I put myself back to sleep.
No, a coma.

  the bells
in all the children's books
  were broken
all the shooting stars fell

out of heaven
and it was forever darkness
and sadness
at night the moon would burn
thereafter
like a rose
that would always belong
to my mother

I had drunk
Medusa's blood,
in the dark,
saw her face,
but,
unlike Perseus,
I became the blind groom
of unfathomable
fascination

After that whenever she began to drink,
I would stay home with her.
She was the moonlight.
She was the darkness.

When my boyhood friends would boast of
seeing so-and-so's panties,
I would go home to be with my mother.

My first arrest took place in junior high school:
a gun.
My second arrest:
a gun, etc.
I was in a club called
The Young Demons.
We were into guns,
drugs and territory.
My life was rehabs,
Arrests and jails
Crabs
Syphilis
Hepatitis

And finally
The mad houses:
These were the walls of insomnia
Where Dante became incontinent and feeble,
Twirling his eighteen inch Asian penis;
Where God sat in an antique electric chair
Preaching the gospel of a heaven made of iron;
Where doctors and lawyers
Burned their faces with lighted cigarettes;
Where human excrement was soap
And patients removed imaginary wires from their throats;
Where the clouds of heaven could be bought for a blow job.

II. INVENTORY

IN MEMORY OF EUGENE PEREZ

(drowned May 25, '62)

Botchy-white balloon-blown
like a rubber ball
the East River coughs you up
clutching holy sea-weed
oil-slicks halo your shriveled mouth

Eels party in the sunken sockets
of your eyes
crabs ear-ring your ears
your soul smells in the river
but your heart hangs in my seclusion room
your blobbed face won't knife your therapist's sleep
St. Peter picks the worms
in your feet

Turno
you got in the wind
I heard your lungs croak on the
11 p.m. ebb
while your ghost strokes
in hell's fish bowl.

THE MEMORY OF BENNY (KID) PARET

to Norman & Carey Bluhm

1

Twelve Bells
        Benny's on the ropes
Twelve Bells
        he has no feet
Twelve Bells
        he can't make gloves
Twelve Bells
        one rope through his head
Twelve Bells
        one rope through his chest
Twelve Bells
        one rope through his leg
Twelve Bells
        a rubber apple in his mouth
Twelve Bells
        his jaw hangs like a moth
Twelve Bells
        his face is a torn flower
Twelve Bells
        his hands fall off the clocks
Twelve Bells
        he's a fly in a glass of milk

2

Little Benny's tears
          wounded pebbles on the
                    coffin lids
    your folded hands
          two dead countries
               in my head
    the rope burns
          cold welts on your back
  your head is a turban
               of bandages
  your eyes are bread
         I can't eat
  the ring is a crib
            where you sleep
Benny's an empty bag.

III. UNDERGROUND WITH THE ORIOLE

INVENTORY—TO 100TH STREET

for John Bernard Myers

In the corner lot
where they parked
green banana tricks
fruits
palmed in paper straw
I smell
bedbug & kitchen-cockroach
summer afternoons

Somewhere
tailless
one-eyed cats
doting in fat garbage cans
screaming with the stench
of rice & beans
strawberry tampax
piled
high as the smell
(I was small & slick)
the covers tilted
like the hat of a rock-look wino
in a deep
knee-bend nod
on a beer
can-street
Sunday morning

There were always
time-thick
empty nights
of nothing to do
but listen to the
ethereal
(she lived on the top floor)
I-go-for-more screams
of Charlie's pimp's woman
when he beats her
for his good

business principles
joy-pop the block
with morning-talk

I hear the dim iron dawn yawning
(I lived on Third Ave.)
rattle
nights into
Saturday morning
flag-bloomer
eclipses
just before the hunt—
they were as big—
the cats
like jungle bunnies
fierce with fleas & sores

I see window-people
hanging out of gooey-stick slips
sweating
strange
below-the-button drawers
crouched junkies in hallways
with monkey backs
eating cellophane bananas
on a g-string
waiting
for that last bust
Spics with cock-comb
hair fronts
ear-gulping mambo music
eye-lapping pepperican flower
crotches

I can hear the streets whispering
in the ears of yelping kids

in the fun-gushing that
rippled my blood
in the pump

but the kids
are dying in the lot
like the tarry-blown feet
of the rain
jingling
on the rusty-green
of yesterday's
fire escapes.

MULATA

to Phyllis

And if I love you, we'll fight.
I'll call you bitch, tack head,
And curse the gods, Lincoln, and the feminists.
Beat you—not too hard, in the right places—
Stuff, I'm a man, no trick!
Laugh, when you cry like a child, hurt . . .
Bite swallow the lump in my throat.
Leave,
Take the money,
Get my belly full of cheap gin & beer;
Head full of good smoke next to a
Greasy, grinny, lipstick whore with
Endless, sympathetic: hum-hum, definitely,
You're right baby—
In the mist of reefer,
Cigarette and stale-green cigars,
In a bar gray with the laughter of
Hustlers, junkies, and steady, stink-finger tricks
Where the scream of the jukebox
Swells the air and makes my brain thick
With forget-you
And then,

The scent of your hair, body,
When you finished cleaning the house—
I found it so delightfully unpleasant,
Sends the blood screaming through my legs for you,
And explodes the tingling blue bubble I'm in . . .
Homesickness of you begins to seep in,
Slowly, cruelly till night skulks away
From sour, headachey dawn.
And if I love you,
I'll wait and beat the ancient seconds of
Without-you-since-yesterday,
As I stumble, back-bent, fumbling for keys,
Chewing Juicy Fruit,
Up the squeaky stair, just to drown you,
Just once more,

In an ocean of fresh new
I'm sorries—baby—darling—honey—please—
And hungry, stale-smoke-liquor kisses,
Gaudy, alien perfumed hugs.
And if I love you, the bitch storm
Passes to the crisp white lap of
Sheets and pillows,
Where I wander in—up—out—down
The chestnut thighbone avenue,
Barely touching, panting, my nostrils
Blowing
On your softsilk body to mine,
A cherry-nostrum wonder—
Experience . . .
BANG!
. . . And if I love you we'll fight again.

HOTEL PARK (EAST 110TH ST.)

My fingers
popping with eyes
touch you
in a sea of foaming sheets

I beauty-mark your blubbery thighs
mash thick kisses
on your swollen lips
your tongue puddles in my ear
I'm king of the ceiling

The bed beehives with sighs
my nose spiders
in your mouse-tit hair
babybottle breasts
dance with the springs
your meshy bush
drips with nightdew
nailed to my loins
like religion

Then grisly seconds clog
the sand-clocks
love's funk hangs
in the room
like a dirty shirt
we leave
but life pools behind
the hairy socket
it smells like a miracle

we're sixteen.

MOM I'M ALL SCREWED UP

Moth-eyed
by the neon signs
I peeped
at the stiff little worms
screwing in your head
spider crabs
crawled in my ear

With popping antennae ringlets
you looked like
a preying mantis
cold cream & turban
science fiction gleam
as real
as cancer
spreading
stuffed-tits-and-rag-guts
yawning
brillo-crotch
that stunk
all over me
playing
Johnny-on-the-pony
on me
indoors

The mattress groaned
I moaned
Mom
I'm no horse
you have pimples on your butt
your belly button droops
your boy pop left
the rose of your hopes
no
no

With lollipop-grin lips
on my solitaire piece
you had no teeth

I'm still scaling scabs of
hot garlic
slob-kisses

isn't mamacita's heart going to
kiss mom
good night
no
no
no.

PRIMAVERA

A mummy
crumbling
in the bar

my eyes
empty mirrors
my kidneys
drunken flowers

Then dawn
an eyelid

I come to you
as always
green
tired
need a shave
a bath
I stink
unlock the nights
in jail
it's spring on the windows
my heart
in a bag
and some beer

Hi Monkey
I'm home

ABUELA'S WAKE

Then her mouth flew open
        like a fish sucking air
                Jesus flipped with a greasy hook
      I wanted to pop a cap in his plaster head

Abuelo laid with her
                        naked
            he blew his nose
                his eyes
                    broken toys
        while he sang her to sleep

I'll tie your cold finger with
ribbons for the wedding ring—
I sold your teeth when I was drunk
Negra Bird-Lips   my heart   your grave . . .

His lips fumbled on her wrinkled breasts
      Mom screamed barbed wire
                in my shoe-high ears
my stickball smile fell off my face

Concha
      the wake's witch
        wearing her mothball smile
          held the black rosary
            like a snake with a Catholic head
                            it still hisses in my bed
    dribbling the wooden words

Dios te salve Maria
Dios te salve Maria

outside
   the mouth of December tinked on the windows

By the stumped candles
     ice-bird white tearing wax
       Abuelo pillowed her head

in the mouse-velvet coffin
smeared her chalk face with
glass kisses & drunken tears
the wreaths were shadows
standing in the corners

Abuelo sits in the kitchen
Abuela's eyes are berries in his head
he drinks her face in Gallo wine
it licks his heart
by the wedding picture
in the empty bedroom

Abuelo
her eyes are pools the rain can't find
she sleeps in a green gown of moss
and tiny paws of dew dress the grave

your heart's a tin cup
begging for wine.

PUDGY

I'd swish through the door
tiptoeing
goofed on speedballs
with a yellow-jaundice twinkle
in my glassy eyes

you'd be waiting in the kitchen
perched on a chair
like Judge Leibowitz
your face mooned
wet thighs
at me

Instead
I'd stash my joints—
in the food-bare freezer
take five
throw off my clothes
drop in bed
like an empty pebble

I'd stink of
catting on roofs & in basements
barnacled with sores & pimples
sweat-starchy sock & greasy underwear
on my back two weeks
you looking top-flight
curlicues of perfume
running through your nesty hair
but I was slimming-off
in sleep
a glazed tear on your chubby cheek
whimpering out
I found a bag of that stuff
in the Bible—
You're never home anymore
aaahhh
shut up—
you're lucky I'm home tonight

and nod back in my bucket
till the monkey
creaked my back awake—
gobble out of bed
fireman my clothes on
pistoled out of the house
after I'd beat you out of your
carfare & lunch money
for my morning fix

I took cures & cures
wrote you letters

we'll start all over
never take off again
clean up for good this trip
you were my first high
cop a slave & work for you only
I'm really getting down in therapy
this time

sign them
Your forever
Loving husband

P.S. I need commissary

on a paper napkin
you wrote
Dear Liar
Come Home.

O my chocolate Princess
I lay in bed
smelling of Lifebuoy soap & toothpaste
light a stogie & watch the smoke
unshoe ghost-nude thoughts

my feet gag my heart
they're cold.

GORILLA

to 1959

Eyes tearing
nose running
then the yawn
and his head
a wreath of ice
with a handful
of raisins for hair
razors & twitches
in his joints
keep him from
the floor
to the cot
and his eyelids
blink like hammers
The cramps in his stomach
double up to his knees
he yawns
and his ribs stick out
like thorns
Call for the hack
he's dying

"Tell him to drink cold
water and walk slow"
the heartbeats hang on the bars
and fall through the tier
like sunlight
Ice him—
let him take to the sheets
and dance with the bulb
"Save it for Sunday and
let them pass the plate"
The catnaps
glassine dreams
of golden cookers
dollar bill collars
hypos—
like glass hummingbirds

in his arms
turn to wood
he yawns
blows his fix
he's awake
and the shadow of the hack
hangs upside down.

EMPTY CAGE

I've been looking at the
old question mark

It screams
while I sleep
whispers
when I walk

It kills
eats
and vomits everything

I want to see
water-colored
walls
in the Tombs

a suede-top nigger
running for
president
not trees.

POEM

To My Father

Iron
Iron

I
Have
Burned
Down
The
Sky.

POEM

My brother
fixed his new
cuff link
to ride the lightning
for murder
and Mom ironed
his clothes
for summer camp

You know how
fussy he is

this morning smelled
like burnt hair

TUESDAY

My heart is a
grasshopper
between your breasts
the bedsheets are winter
we cling to each other
the walls are on fire

My nose is in your ribs
your lips in my hair
the moon
a red lip-print
in your navel
and your legs
two black highways
around my neck

Your eyes are filled
with ponies & stars
your body
a carnival flower
where naked nuns
crawled in my ear
crowned with pin drops
of sweat
dance in my head

SHOE

May these
roses keep
the secret
when I hold
You
there's an
old lamp
burning
up
side
down
in my heart
O my love
the fumes
go to my head

I prefer
your
toe.

BEACH

There
happy as a greenfly
toes popping out
like corks in the sand
Buddhas on stilted chairs
ocean tattooed with
bathing caps
mud castles
seashell windows
and sunglasses staring
at the panty-blue sky
webbed seaweed
windblown
brown
on an eel-green
bottle

On the meat line
sun sprays of iodine
on fish-white backs
wide splits
heavy squats with cat whiskers
I'm the ocean between their legs
my toetips cling to the seashore
sea gulls whirlpool in my hair
and sing in my windy ear
O Beach
heaven of dark-eyed belly buttons
you tricked-off the seashells
for Trojan-floats & beer cans.

HAIKU

for Frank O'Hara

I
The lights are out
The cats are hungry
The room is full of gangsters

II
The dishes are dirty
The icebox is empty
I dream of celery and a compass

III
The roof is upstairs
The window next door
A guitar in the shower

IV
The hours disappear in my room
Where is my blue pistol
The door-god is knocking.

THE WOMAN

Today I met my woman in the subway . . . it was winter.
She wore a red coat down to her knees with a black
fur collar. I could only see the back of her head,
which was blue because of the kerchief & the flower
she wore. She wasn't facing me. Her shoes were
orange and her stockings black. I went up to her
and said I had found a little part of her in all
the women I have ever known, and I have always loved her.
I told her: "We can make it & crib together . . .
things won't be too bad . . . life is a snap!"

Then she turned to me. Her face was sea-brown; her
lips were thick; her eyes were dried wells and the
flower in her hair was plastic. I said to her that
I loved her more than ever now and must know her name
because she was what life was about. She grinned:
her teeth were stubs of jade. I kissed her and sucked
her lips. She said any name would do. . . . I called her
My Woman and I took her hand. It was like old dried
wood with cracks in it; her knuckles were cold lumps
I pressed to my face.

She unbuttoned her coat. Her body was black and her skin
was wrinkled and stuck to her bones like tape. She had
no breasts; they were eaten away by cancer I guess.
My hands were filled with warm and slippery flesh.

She kicked off her orange shoes and asked me to kiss
her feet . . . they were small and her toes were chewed
stubs. I said I would kiss them if only she would give
me her heart. She said she would in exchange for mine.
I told her my heart was young and full, filled with
flowers, birds, and perfumed tears, but if she wanted it
she could have it.

The train came to a sudden stop. It was spring. I fell
away from her across the aisle dreaming of wreaths. She
dropped her heart and kicked it over to me. I took it . . .
it was a coffin filled with dry worms. I ran off with it, as
happy as a faggot in boy's town.

THE WELDER

to David Smith

I

He is gliding on her like a block of ice
On an iron stove

I am from a distant land

He gave her a brick
Cut off her hair
It is falling
She is sinking

I have walked in front of buildings
Put your hand in the sunlight on the maps
Your head in the river
We will live in the sea
Or your hair

Falling
Your lips are red like snow
Indian head   Orizaba   Mexican Beer

II

She is learning like a Russian bird
The early smells
Surrounding like landslides
Her fingers skating near my arm
I am gliding

I once lived in Havana

III

A thin lamp in my hand
A scrim

The third act is a shadow crossing a child
They are glass
The clown is in love with the lock
On her wrist

She is rushing against my hands
The flowers are sinking in the room like ether

IV
Our bodies are fish trembling in gelatin

I turn my waist
A machine
To the tip of your cheek
A circus

I am living in your stockings
Volcanoes

V
A green cigarette
A purple mouth
A factory
Quick
                    Safar

VI
My hands are surrounding
Your calendar
A sunflower
One foot across

I turn my waist
A green cigarette

The sea is sinking
With figures in her hair
A purple factory of lead suns
On your cheek

The sharks are melting in
The snow like volcanoes

A glacier suffocating a siren.

SPANISH POETRY

There is nothing left but a change in the room
And you are changing with it like the voices in the next room

You emerge like towers into the smoke
With uncompromising love dipped into water
Then there is nothing left
But the sentries on the walls

What are we building today?
Perhaps something of importance
Because I have raced through the wind to find the end
Your life's stories have no consequence on the earth
It is much too small where you are

This is not the end in your case
Because you are one of the people who will remain for some time
You will meet Valentino and lay yourself by his clay feet
And wipe his tears with your white wings.

SKY—
SARA

although the sky is soft
and I am in love with
the rim of the world

I think of your walk
and I will say to you
how I love you
and the wind from
your cigarette

I will touch your hands
and they will dream
of what we are
and they will wait
for us like the wind
between them

a flame runs over us
and we grow larger than the sky
and we are lost in an idea
and I shall tell you of my life
and of the fires that touch me
each afternoon

nov. 15/69

ODE TO LOVE

My island is trouble:
I have found wet grass in my armpits
and yellow paint in my navel since you left

Do you believe in a cold sane reality?
love is love like a mountain in the room
with a common cold so take my head
I am a wandering snowshoe at your feet

I cannot sleep there is sand in my shoes
there is a wine spot in my dreams that makes me dizzy
I feel like a cloud in the Pacific Ocean stunned by the weather
like an old cover on a new book in your hands
if I were a fur coat you could not get me off in case of fire
I'm interested in the finer things in life
like swimming to Australia in a heat wave
in my arms with only salt between us
we will stop smoking for days on end in our journey
you make me restless when you use up all the air around us
I feel like a gorilla in a chocolate shower
when we watch the sun go down for the last time
if I were lost on this island I would send you my
heart on a raft with some lunch and a love letter:

"My Dearest I am lost."

I am needed here like the sky needs air traffic therefore
I am bored with the idea of life without you on this planet
I want you to be my room deodorant my favorite stone
O ship of love I wish you would blow up
when I think of internal motivation I think
of my liver on rainy days when it hurts
poets are really nice people they're like giant trees
full of sap!

O sun sun my life has not been a drag after all
I could have been a number in a marble game

When I think of you I can spare myself from sleep
I can be as loyal as Blue Cross and as silly as this poem
I am killing my ash tray with an overdose of butts
when I talk to my ash tray about you it gets bored
my subjects are monotonous so it tells me
That's life ash tray.

I will wrap myself in toothpaste every morning and bring
you your favorite coffee for I will be your cup
how can I become famous when I am so distracted?

There is a tiny creep in the room that steals my cigarettes
I won't kill him because I'm in love and nothing else matters
but love on this gorgeous Earth that we're on
this wonderful trap
Anyhow I feel like an overcrowded greenhouse when
you're around.

ODE TO LOVE—PART 2

(litany)

"I am alone in New York I am the mud
from heaven I have distracted this
society with the filth of my life
I have pumped and polluted the streets
with my determinations I have willed
my will with a monotonous infamy
Destroy yourself if you don't know!
I speak from a terrible inner place
before the beginning of my birth
I have been the unnatural vigor of
dreams the meditations of the insane
and the model of the dead my dreams
are countries in another city in hotels
with solitary radios with eyelids and
lipstick on the thread of life for a
dollar I have slaughtered my loins for
a fake and for the scandal in my body
in pursuit of love and my life I take
this for myself with no qualms with no
discretion for I do not fear my blood
any longer or the minerals in my body
before an instant death surrounded by
criticism and chaos waiting for a final
star in a room for a glittering tear
on the floor the color of heaven for I have
been my own somnambulist saint the invention
of my nerves love has been a temporary lift
from nostrils and navel-sucking and from the
petty boredom of a hot body around the channels
of my waist in some emergency!" O fuck who cares.

But it is Sunday and I have come through without a scratch
or a watch to tell you of that time or anyone for that
matter my excitement is your short black hair lighting your
cigarettes over a dinner table or holding your hand in the
theater or saying nothing when we're together on an island
on a magic ocean in the mornings.

This is what I have my new life and a beach full of cabbage
so we can be alone in this mad world of silly images I
promise you 80 years more of life because I feel like a
watermelon covered with Jergens Lotion! I am mad to think
these things but it is a good and kindly madness that will
do the world some good.

I have lived with a broken heart since I can remember since
Webster wrote his wonderful book to Mary if I stop writing
I'll go out like a light and wake up in another marathon
or another life dreaming of you I need coffee.
Someone has put a hand in my coffee if it were yours I don't
think I would stir it for fear of dying of my own perspiration
if you suddenly appeared in my room nude how would you go
back if I drank the coffee? That's life's baby.

Men cry because they do not have the will to live I wonder if
living is a sideline if you're not in love? I wonder about a
lot of things like how you take a shower how you grin when
you brush your teeth how you feel when you think of me
as the only man in the world like me?

Well the time has come to clip my nails and play one last
piece and settle with the Earth for a night and a token of
love your love and the nourishment of a dream with you your
eyes like growing flowers your flowers the vegetations of
Spain a great sadness if you will it on the world.

sunday, sept. 7/69

CANTO

sara

1
below—
the two of us

2
the snow takes us through the snow
and we are spotless

wednesday, feb. 3/70
east 5th street

SARA

9:30

I
love
you
because

I
love
spoons

may 14/70

RIVER

I am furious
like a city
of rumors
I look at
my feet
and see
children
O sun
O sun
I have
put light
ning thru
my hands
whoever
finds me
will be
beautiful
I will be
plentiful
like the
rocks
to see my
father nude
discover
our fingers
the avalanche
between us
my pure figure
image of life
adore me!
adore me!

SARA

I move
over
your
birth
and
breathe
deeply
I love
the world
and
feel
your
touch
I pray
to
animals
and
flee
I
linger
above
you
and
smell
I must
put my
self
out
early
with
your
finger
and lean
my elbows
over you.

july 6/70
east 5th street

IV. ANGEL

159 JOHN STREET

It will rain forever here
the buildings will be turned down
the artist will obscure the weather
the potters and the weavers
will rub the edges of the sand and
a wolf will come to the door
to explain the facts of my life

without illusion our jaws will lock
because it is a common attitude

when you limp
I think of your waterfall larger
than my birth

there are no essentials
about my life
the doctor was ugly
and the nurses were beautiful
a myth to the contrary is a lie.

NATASHA

to My Daughter

When your tongue slipped into the world
like a drop of light I thought of mirrors
and the fantasy of numbers

If the world would change
we would take our clothes off
and allow each other the words
of a whore in love with her reflections

I follow my delirium from room
to room and I am cured of life
like the thinker of fire
the father of all liquids.

THE HUNTER

". . . they murder the air . . . "
—Martha Graham

I will check my gun at the door
and speak to you about life:
Will you merge with me like
skid marks in winter?

I have a small motor I want to give to you.
I know you are under orders,
and I hate the eagles in your heart,
but I do not want to bury you.

Tomorrow is the day
we'll sleep together
with the New England
snow in the belly of
the house—

I have been sighted fifteen miles away.
Just tell me how to stop.
Killing someone is like emptying an ashtray.
I have no excuses I am shaped like a knife.

The giant tells me I need rest because I am cheap.
I am prepared to turn in my skin
although you have one leg.

I have stored up a thousand hours of life.
I hate suicide.
I dial the phone and speak to paragraph
two or three maybe like 16:
"How to keep your eyes open or closed
If you come you won't go blind."

My teeth are set at night like lovers.
I admire your clear life
But you never remember your dreams.
I undress mine one at a time.

The hills are always there like women
I never touch and in the middle there is
always dusk like the lines of order.

I hold my hand at the bottom of the river
and look at the holes in my stomach.
I begin to run through the sky
like the target of a corpse.

HUNTER MOUNTAIN

The sky has the luxury of going anywhere.
The roads follow with the
gratitude of being abandoned
and watch the deer run through smoke.

This is the day of the animals' feeding on our waste,
the fatality of hands passing a soft spot,
the heavy breathing of small yellow animals.
This is my infancy:
three hours from New York,
a fall flexing of odors,
the desperate hunger in a car that sucks the air.

The expectancy of a garden full of wolves,
the face of a tiger in an ashtray.
I move and lie against someone
and plant light where I am correct.

This is the perfect place.
My children spin like bottles
because I am able to lie.
I smile in terror when they touch me.
The facts of my life remain facts.

I offer the guests no memories, no seasons.
The rusted cities of the sea gulls wash ashore
in some cocktail party like a large bird.
Have I stood over you with yellow eyes?
I was prowling your stark white floors
at the bottom of the cage
with such brilliance that I have given up sleep.

I have run through my lungs
down down down into the water
where the fish bring light to the sun
waiting for the weakness of a dreamer.

OPHELIA/OCTOBER '71

I apologize to rusty water
I lost my confidence in the ambulance
When you revealed the history of the
Infancy of your king and of your assassin
Blue green and purple
But you must remember
Mice crawl around the stars and enter their own dreams
And stalk the toys on the floor.

LOBSTER

for Chef René Verdon

The Maine lobster is the most famous of all the shellfish. These creatures gave birth to an extraordinary planet that was able to produce one million different species of lobsters and 350,000 different kinds of humans. The lobster lives and dies, struggles and adapts, and all the while deepens the ocean to preserve the imagination of the universe:

> perhaps some ten billion light-years away,
> when comets were flies, supernovae frogs,
> the galaxies were born; and in this tiny speck
> the dream of this crustacean was a strange,
> wonderful, and improbable eater.

So cold was the dream in spots that the temperatures plunged to -140°F and the iciest lobster grew 9,200 feet thick. So warm was the dream that the temperature reached 138° in the shade where it flourished at depths of six miles, before the eaters moved onto the land.

The lobsters grew wings, making possible a variety of vegetation from tiny flowers to massive woods that resisted the face of the earth. And in one of nature's most amazing creations, the lobsters stepped out of the shower dripping wet and into the machines that move at the bottom of the sea, where they beat each other with bay leaves, vinegar, and wine.

Lobsters are like old men in the bathhouses who dream of Vulcan and varicose veins. The lobsters appear to be hot balloons that frighten the kiss of death. But they know the kiss of death is going bald in fine restaurants: and one can notice, just off center, the fine white laugh of the lobster.

THE CHILDREN OF G-2

The children ride out to meet the clouds on Easter Morning. To them the clouds were written in China, and the black ink is not unusual. They are perfect and beautiful, the way the sun should be. On the other side of the world the children hide their radios from cowboy music, but on the other side of the world cowboy shirts are not blue, and against the sky the flames are birds in their fingers. When it rains the moonlight turns into a rubber duck and the duck becomes the water not needing swans because the swans are submarines that float between you and me.

These are the stories when you learn to smoke like the lion tamer without a cock, or the violinist without a rose. To them the flames are all the same except for the ones that look like a refrigerator. When you open the refrigerator it lights up the room, and when you write poetry it goes hungry and the screams are like magic. You become the frightened customer who drinks too much, and the martinis think of the winos who no longer play cards when the robins are on parade to the worms. Soon the worms are singing to the resurrection of your liver and ignore the robins, the winds of March, and the holidays.

THE UNDERWORLD

This beautifully marked insect has a bright yellow body with black wings and a forehead. It sings clear and strong but can no longer fly in a smooth pattern near the ground. In the spring it goes unmarked and pale blue. It ranks high among men and is malodorous and reddish as were the stone men. During the war there was a bizarre incident: The idea was that the insects would transmit the yips of enemy soldiers. The plan was fascinating but had to be abandoned.

This insect is possessed of sexual powers, and the typical male copulates at dawn in every way possible. The male comes near a couple who are mating and he becomes terribly excited. He punctures the abdomen of the female. This development had no reason. In fact, they have no limits of irregularity. But the African species are developing facial muscles that indicate emotions.

AZALEAS

Mountain azaleas grow in the woods as most fragrant flowers. But this species is similar to the future. The flower stalks are glandular and sticky, and their characteristics vary greatly. The leaves are arranged neatly showing a bright yellow with a thick neck that grows 8 1/2 inches in one hour. This sacklike substance is suspended in the shade of fruit trees. The eggs are white with streaks of sand and, unlike ivory azaleas, are tempted to dry the universe.

TULIPS

They are dressed in white and hold beakers up to the sun. For this variety there is no hope of dawn since they roll over the moon. They want to become part of a single body, bound to each other by physical connections such as the exchange of glands, their secretions giving order to their mates; and they spend the last part of their lives feeding glands, although this was not always so.

GERANIUM

On quiet nights the screech of the geranium is mournful and is not noticed in the orchards or in the natural environment of the magnificent clouds. The deliberations of this flower are powerful horns that may curl in a full circle. In a sense, they are living fossils as big as Alaska. The geranium listens to mountains and gunfire and waits for the male, who is slightly smaller and the most voracious of the underwater animals: It is the male geranium whose bones are left for the holidays.

VIOLETS

The continent grows two to three feet high
with its elaborate flowers, several hundred
species of violets:
the violets create vigorous new forms
and spread patches of color when the
blond appears on the floor,
like a small hole full of yellow and white
and if you cut yourself don't lose an eye
she will place a violet in the socket
and insist that violets have memories.

FROM "DRACULA TO THE ANGELS"

As a result of spring the mosquitoes are magnificent.
From the point of view of the air they are unfathomable.
—we don't deserve them—

Mosquitoes are accustomed to considering themselves
perfect
This year they will withdraw
With a mouthful of poets.
Poets are to mosquitoes what cigarettes are to lung cancer:
There are too many poets and not enough mosquitoes.
To the mosquitoes it's a matter of survival:

1. a poet sees an owl and he thinks of a woman's crotch—
2. a mosquito sees a poet and he thinks of a woman's
crotch—

Poets and mosquitoes have one thing in common—
They suck.

EL BRONX

I hate the Orient in the morning. The kisses are too slow,
like the breaking of smallpox and the women who have
three tits struggle from one continent to another:

Everything trembles in this building when the lovers fuck.
They think they're putting the salt back in the sand. And
the tenants wonder about the dogs at dawn that rest like the
wind on a gleaming taxi. Why should I leave this swamp?
The showers are relentless, and the water is always hot, as
hot as the three small closets that we have full of shoes
worshipping the small clouds of underwear, the butterflies
of smoke.

SCENARIO

for Edwin Denby

The curtain rises and the stage is dark. An alarm clock is heard and the stage becomes brightly lit. The stage is divided.

STAGE RIGHT

A huge alarm clock is seen, a huge bed, chair and full-length mirror, and other large objects that are found in a bedroom. There is a figure in the bed.

STAGE LEFT

A dance studio with mirrors in the background and life-size or larger-than-life sculptures or paintings of legendary great dancers. Young dancers, wearing brightly colored leotards, are frozen in a tableau.

THE DANCE

EPISODE I

Edwin cheerfully bounces out of bed wearing a pale raincoat. He dances around the bed, the clock, and the other large objects in the room as if to greet then, ending in front of the mirror where he strikes the exaggerated poses of a fashion model. He gracefully takes off the raincoat, throws it on a chair and then stretches many times. He holds his hands up to the mirror and examines them carefully, revolving them in the air like an Indian dancer.

EPISODE II

While Edwin is examining his hands, the dance students suddenly come to life with quick, erratic, jerky motions. Edwin enters the studio and with a sweep of his hands stops what they are doing and gently admonishes them. He proceeds to teach them the formal dance. He shows them various steps and stances, but never gives them the opportunity to follow any of his examples. Instead he dances and dances around them, and the dance students mock him by bowing and clapping politely. They thank him and he dismisses them. They leave. Edwin is bewildered and sad as he returns to his room. He walks to the mirror, holds his hands up and examines them carefully, revolving them in the air like an Indian dancer.

EPISODE III

As Edwin enters the room, the lights are dimmed and a young couple enter the studio furtively. They are wearing pale raincoats. The young man takes his raincoat off and then takes the raincoat off the young girl. At this moment, Edwin takes the raincoat off an imaginary dancer in his room. The young couple begin to dance. Edwin dances with his invisible partner doing the same dance. The young couple stop. Edwin stops. The young man takes his raincoat and drapes it on his and her shoulders; simultaneously, Edwin puts his raincoat on. The lights become dimmer as the young couple kiss and leave the stage. Edwin goes to bed.

CURTAIN

CHIN CHOW

Just before twelve the large shoe was quiet,
the ends of its hair were rough,
and as white as the human race
gigantically in love with a bar of soap.
Until 1965 the advance of the Chinese meant nothing
But a cold beer and a take-out menu.

CUAUHTEMOC

This knife is as long as my wife in the pool
and I am as dark as the sun
The silence from the moon is as dark when we sleep

I always bring my captives here
and let the grapevines choke them

The stars will crash and last for years
I grin at them and give them fruit
I am an expert at my job
I am their home

I spend the morning writing letters
while the machines crush the priest
I remember their flat runways
when they stripped for weddings

It was the death of all the warriors
and their enemies
When the wind screamed around their feet
I would listen to my knife

It was the time to pull their hearts out
and give them to the children

I have given them the wings to heaven
and they are my last legend
frozen like the hands of a small monkey

We call their last sounds the wind
This sound brings us childhood
as if it were life
These are the days of our calendar

Our children pray to them
and play with their hearts with sticks
We pray to the children and their sticks
and it rains for hours on the crops

Lightning makes the trees smell like my knife
As long as the heart is quiet we are waterproof

I am the king of the shade in the green jungle
The people hurry to see my accidents
The mothers among them hold their children
up to me as *ixiptlas*

Their small bones make very little noises
and their small eyes will become
beans for Texcatlipoca

They exchange gifts
Some of them have not seen
each other since the last rain.

CHILE

to Humberto Diaz-Casanuevas

The vast Asian stars
in the empty house
freeze a bird
until it is safe.

On a spot of blood
in the little city
we shoot the birds
in the back.

PATCHOULI

it's only that I think of you
as a wagon
or a mule with legs that
point to the stars

or a soft language
waiting to stroke a mirror
in a swamp

everyday is a new instrument
lavishly completed
like a part-time cane

the language of night is a prosperous sheet
full of delicate assumptions

the language of night is fragile
like a warm net full of rumors

I want to give you a box of signatures
that include all my perfect moments.

YELLOWSTONE

Before I tell you
of the stars
that keep you awake

like the thin jets
that hunt the buffalo

I want to stand in
front of you with
my gang of dreams

The ones that make
the mountains lose
their power.

POSTCARD

You must forgive me, it is my new life in the fog.
My errors disappear like magic from their own exhaustion,
and I want to forget the furniture of complicated women.
Well, the history of the sun moves farther into the west;
below the mountains you can see the stones in a bottle of
brandy that breaks the heart of the ocean. —Frank

PLENA

During the day I play at drowning
looking for the smoke
of eyelashes and faded hair
the lilac shadows of blood
and the ruins of coffee
but at night
I dream of the last syllable
in my mother's heart
the last red word in her lungs.

½ SONNET

The storms of ice in the handkerchief
arrive
like the horses of the river
and the powder of the sea
when the fish turn to Portugal
looking for the angel of the sonnets
the pebbles of the prince of darkness.

V. YEAR'S END

YEAR'S END

I
When I pause, anemones fall on the month of December.
And I am foolish enough to answer the phone, like a drop
of water sliding across a linen tablecloth, falling
on the lap of a lover. I have,
in my hand, the channel of sovereign energy, the quiet
continent that hardens into soil. A fine Minnesota rain
falls on the swans that have given their wet bread to
the enemy in the pool. What shall I bring tomorrow?

II
Nature's caricatures have left us the tender sounds
of a throat in mourning for the throbbing of the Earth.
So we ascend through our afflictions to catch a fleeing
thought, the loveliest of the airs between us. A hand is lost
in the Oblivion. How many thoughts does it take to make
a century? Life, with all its evenings,
religiously returns each morning like
a mountain opening up within the heart.

III
I suspect when I pause on the month of December
anemones fall.
Dear sacred heart, each Friday I crawl away from your soft
leather orchid that shatters my soul with its dark
shudders of moonlight.

PISCES

Cesar Vallejo was born March 15, 1892, in a small
mining town in northern Peru. In the spring of 1938
he developed a fever the European doctors could
not diagnose or treat, and he died in Paris on April
15, 1938, while it was raining. Like a great fish,
Vallejo rolled back into the sea
the stone of a gentle hunchback.

SERMO I

for Humberto Diaz Casanueva

We live as a family
the oldest in the center
we die slowly
bury our dead between the
trees and gesticulate
angrily when the trees
try to uproot them

THE HISTORY OF NIGHT

Night falls at different speeds and at the center
there are drops of rain. Not far from
the bed meteorites
thinly coat the entire universe.
The zodiac floats into icicles that form
our passing glances.
Should the sun throw more light on glimmering
autumn, the leaves would
shut our arms that dangle in the wind.
There is no time for comedy;
every stone regains hope and dies immediately.

NOTES TO A ROOM

Along the road the poem is out of control, like the
wandering spirit of a candle.
A lovely black figure enters the
room, caring little for fragile birds, and nurses the temperature
of the yellow book marker halfway down the page. A simple
opening in the suffocating book that shines modestly when
tossed away. But we are so brand new, with no hope of ever
returning except on an occasional night.

WINTER POND

for Christophe de Menil

A tulip dives into the icy water to find a fish.
It swims in and out of the reflections
of the mountains.
It shows a kind of agitation that circulates
in the water.
The ripples move toward the forehead of the viewer.
The tulip goes swimming
not in search of the fish
but of the viewer's soul.
To the tulip the viewer's soul is flat like the
face of a child.
The soul prefers a small bed of ashes inside a whale.
The tulip has no memory.
The fish continue to watch the horizons of the earth
glide into the arctic flowers.

THE HAND

The hand is all heart. It hops around like a toad to prove its dexterity. It presses your pockets on cold winter days and, in its profound state, polishes an apple for you. Silently it waits in the subways when it rains and is more of a hand than ever. It emerges from your humid coat, like a swollen hyena with its rancorous juices, to offer the young lady next to you a flat heart. Of course you get a slap and someone's boring hand dials the police, who arrive with fat hand . . .

The hand requires few words. It howls, repels odors and keeps the body of its lover from becoming slippery. A drop of water splashes in the crater of its palm, Merlin's pure lapis in the middle of the night. The lover's hand imagines itself a lover in the flabbiness of a perspiring torso, rolling in the wash of sighs. Armless, the hand spanks and slides around the mass of the sexual object with giant fingers that appear like rubber slugs in the moonlight.

MY HEART

My heart is the shyest object in the world. It has numerous
qualities carelessly mixed together and insectlike roots that can
perceive the entire universe in an instant. It blushes when
it dies or becomes a monster when it loves. Imagine
the size of it when you undress. It becomes a periscope
each spring. It would like to be a lighthouse instead of being
in my chest. It is blind to joy and obligation, and in solitude,
threatens to burst. It is an expensive organ just inches
away from my mouth and thinks of itself as a praying mantis
or a phantom without a head. Gravity confuses it when I am
alarmed, and it would worship the sun on a stone.
When I sleep it is in a state of permanent repentance
and sinks to the bottom of my churning dreams.

SLEEP

Sleep grows agile and slippery with the coming of life.
Yet it is mediocre, as a pebble. Sleep has its peculiar
dignity, lives alone, ignores the force of nature and
would melt before your eyes rather than be caressed.
It is docile, and smooth when it rubs against your pants,
like a magic stone in the subway. The more you dream,
the more it explodes, shattering all things into a
single night. Beginning with perfect control, it will
occupy your nights, will offer you the utter lie of fire,
and the generosity of clean hands.

DISSERTATION

The face endures like a sponge while
the flabby eyes conduct a study of
the world. The body is only a speechless
muscle filled with water.
We avoid covering it with marks and
treat it like bread. Rain does not
touch the body because it knows
nothing of pleasure. But the pill
adores the body and cannot sleep
without it. This is a familiar
practice of the human race: to form
a crust around the earth as if the
Alps were fingernails around a bowl.
This is what the body does
when it moves in one direction.
One can only compare it to a goat,
and we have the nerve to consume the goat.

ON POETRY

Below me my feet are persistent, the marks on them
are whispers. Of course they do not respond to my obsessions.
My obsessions collapse in order to sacrifice themselves.
One might almost say I'm mad because I humble myself
before gravity. The table I write on is stubborn.
It defies gravity with its four legs and would sooner laugh at me.
The definition of obsession is a pathological anxiety,
fearsome, devious, that flirts with water. It is the exclusive
influence of poetry. The poet's instability makes him obedient
to a sheet of paper, and the slightest stir creates a small factory
like childbirth and human stupidity. Poetry is pinker
than nature, devastates every heart but owes itself nothing.
It does not require air and is not agile. The face of poetry
is an expressive cut of meat that gives us a glimpse of truth.

CADUCEUS

At the heart of the scalpel reasoning is desperate and elusive,
always seeking tragic information. The scalpel would rather be
a leaf on a dog's ear than encounter an energetic muscle or the
disoriented air. Yet it rejects the depths of the body as a
lover and would rather hide in a wicker basket and tempt the
cobra into love. But the cobra is meditative, turning thoughts
into eternity, and is suspicious of the scalpel's discreet
advances. The spirit of the scalpel is a platitude and the
heart of the cobra is a seashell that is stirred by shiny
things in the darkness. Only one word is acceptable to both—
blood. Each surrenders to the Danube and all the waters that
follow. To both this is the terrible flavor of love. In fact
it is only after their seductions that the bitterness begins.
The archaic release of the cobra's passion disturbs the bright
scalpel and it would like to hide in Neptune's ancient heart.
In truth, both are polite and supply infinity with corpses.
For each is capable of successive convictions.

NEW YORK

The streets have become unrecognizable.
The entire city is in tears and surrounded by water.
In the harbor a lovely hand appears.

SUNFISH

No one should shine or need an umbrella in hell
or lose his voice in a dream or have to ask
in the middle of the night:

"I am in the deepest part of my body
when you uncoil underneath the blanket";
I move into the kitchen
onto the small antique chair with enormous wings
like a shotgun full of ice.

And I read the book of ivy and
enter the red river
under the influence of the sun.

POEM FROM AMOR

There are no bones in poverty and
pain. You advise me to write poems of
insanity, poems of a face eternally hidden

by laughter. Spain's greatest architect
slept with you a quarter
of a century ago. Now I am your youngest poet, and

fill your bed with ink. In the other world, in
other words, I threw away my shoes looking
for you on the throat of a

flower. The eyes of the brolacchan lack
the great gentleness of paradise. And I live in the vague
terror you will call and offer me a summer song and coffee.

VOYAGERS

When poets love each other from across the page
occasionally they whisper in the same room
and gather their poems like unborn faces in the dark.
They speak in codes of rubber sandals in the shower
while rubbing away the shadow of soapy water
and when they kiss
things fall out of their pockets.

THE FUTURE

There is
A white fish turning on its stomach
Pressing great things against my pants
Like an animal made of snow
It would be terrible if I were the sun
Melting her on everyone
Season after season
I am born a son
What if after
So much eternity
I outlived her?
My son would be the darkness
Between the seasons
The imitations of moonlight
No
He would be the fortune teller's mirror
In a coffee cup
The last hallucination of the hunted fox.

TO PEDRO FLORES DIAZ
my Grandfather

Winter and milk are like flocks of birds
And dreams are the wives of the world
And as long as women go on washing
They will leave their dust to cover
The marks of men
My grandfather married the winter
The one with the big red heat
The one that looked like milk in the dark.

LOLA

my Grandmother

Ivory ripens
Like salt
On a doorknob.

MACHU PICCHU

When the blue islands hurried
South to die on the white beaches
You were created
Out of joy and sorrow
Out of the law of pain
And circumstance
According to ancient formulas

My son
A small desert on his mother's
Sleeping breast
The other life that hugs the tides
A descendant of salt
Burning in his sleep.

UN POCO LOCO

after Larry Fagin

I want to eat everything you are wearing
your dark red feathers
your doorbell
the ant farm in your poems
the little red hair in your watch.

MAIZ

The only bitter thing
About my father is
His dreams
Elegant ears of corn
The offertory of the earth
The fertility of rustic organs
And the iron lush of future ruins

Anger makes an afternoon a child
And the sorrow of the world a scar

Nine female clouds chant in anger
My father's death was a snowflake
In the river
His beard covered
The light poetry of the catafalque
As the insects of the world carried
Him to catch up with the day.

VI. TULUM

A LOGRO DECIRTE

Another unconsummated morning
in our consecrated bed
no magic sulfur this morning
no scratched and naked heart
no bleeding bed
when we awoke this morning
with our dark dreams intact

I shower
shave
change
my heart
because
the other one belongs to the animal I gave you
the one from the sea
the one that thought you were a wave
the one that wanted to be a drop of water on your
skin.

September 5, 1993

EL LOBO

There is a wolf among the stars
looking for
your eyes
your hands
your mouth
to be with you forever
to be your mountain
to give you its hungry rivers

why does the wolf suffer?

because it is not a man
because the rivers climb up the mountain
because love laughs between night and day
because I am waiting for you
my pale angel
like salt
in my small life.

September 6, 1993

TULUM

Do you remember
the island we met
on our honeymoon

it wore a crown of gold
for you
when you walked
upon it
your feet lost their leaves
marking the sands forever
and the Mayan green waters
flourished when you
finally
stepped into my life

we occupied the hotel room
the one that waited for you
since last year
when we blessed it
with sand
with souvenirs
the ocean keeps
for us in its arms
until it grows old
watching us sleep

do you remember Arturo
who each year
greets us
with the keys to our room
and tells us
that the island is well
that the island will grow more flowers
because you will walk upon it
that the ocean will shed its frown
when it joins you
each morning for your swim
that the moon will appear tonight
to give you a drop of its blood

that all the new born stones
await your secret kiss
to build the wall of the world
to contain
my love
for you
my beloved
my love

This is our island
our coral
gleaming
with the naked things
I adore
in the mornings
where my tongue
lives
with your skin
in the happiest
house on earth

this slender strip of sand
with its ruins
devours our movements
on its beaches
it shall wait for us each November
as autumn departs in the north
seeking our island
our nights of sand
where the sky makes no sound
as it gathers our salt
to catch
our departing
kisses.

October 30, 1993

VII. ORFEO

LA ONDA

February 8, 1994

When you comb your hair
and look at me

the wings in your eyes
move slowly around the world

looking for my mouth
leaving my pillow in peace

I close my eyes
I chose endless love

because I cannot live
without falling to earth

with its caresses
with its rough fires

my dear love

I will not sleep
without the world spinning

between us creating
summer and watermelons

that is what I want
when you comb your hair

and I close my eyes.

THIS IS A POEM ABOUT MY LIFE

February 14, 1994

the grapes
remind me of the whales
gathering salt in the ocean

this is a poem about my life

you've interrupted
my life and death schedule
which gives me that poetic look each day

this is a poem about my life

where was I before I met you?
I was eroding on my way to work
and slept a lot
deep in the subways

this is a poem about my life

then I met your lips
on that windy day
I stopped poisoning my life
on Monday mornings

this is a poem about my life

when I met you
you were undressed
like a stone in the rain
I swam after utterly naked

this is a poem about my life

before you leave me to heal
I will find you someone to love
who will be shaped like a box

this is a poem about my life

before you leave me to heal
I will become an apple
and hide in a clock

this is a poem about my life

I will plant these wild lines
they will grow into honey
and weep in the spring
for you

TE AMO

February 17, 1994

when I think of you
each day
is my daily bread
and a little sea
of peas in my soup

HANDS

February 18, 1994

our hands are infants
that need our loving care

hands cry
and grow
like children

I once knew a yellow hand
who died alone without a hand

I've seen hands
hunting for bread

I've seen hands
lie to the sky

some hands speak
in the dark

some hands strangle
another hand in prayer

there are poets
with big hands

there are hands
who have forgotten
their names

there are women
who won't touch
a hand

there are hands
that come and go

I'm a professor
of hands

there is no universe
without your hands

I'M TIRED

February 21, 1994

I want you to grow old with me

i.e. to catch up to me
as I am becoming increasingly weary
of writing poems to you

the poems have
discolored my life

I'm tired of the mysterious truth
after I touch you
I'm tired of not knowing what you think about
I'm tired of women who have the same name as you
they don't know that I'm tired of them too

I'm tired of the telephone
of its beige lips
telling me they love me
and that you don't
that you're a figment
in my ear

I don't want my poems to wear out anyone else again
I don't want to die and have this machine at
my bedside holding my hand
draping me with its affectionate black ribbon
wondering who will turn it on when I'm gone
wondering if my soul will become a kiss again.

THINGS COULD BE WORSE

March 2, 1994

the authorities have
the opportunity to do well

things could be worse

in this case I'm the authority
while I'm writing

things could be worse

I'm condemned to walk
and run and chase pigeons off our terrace

things could be worse

I could be an apple
in a pig's mouth

things could be worse

or a shoe looking for a foot
to pound the earth forever

things could be worse

I could be a pair of hands
in my ex-wife's pockets

things could be worse

and stuck with her
in the middle of the ocean

things could be worse

I could still be married to her

MARCH '94

March 6, 1994

I almost slept in my sleep
I almost had a dream
that the rain fell asleep
and dreamt of leaves and wind

it's good to be a dreamer
in March watching the snow comb
the city
watching the bundles move
on their way to work
the nuns tunneling the snow
trying to reach the children
before the light changes to red

the crabs spread salt on the eels
that move the buses
the gods of gloves and coats
watch the year fall to pieces

I'm dreaming of coats
of their secret women
of their children
hidden in their gloves

I have nothing on my mind
except the stillness of the queen
her winter hair
her glass heart
her white tears
become snow when
the sun breaks her heart

the stars sailing in the sky
undressing the clouds
as the snow leaves its history
on the city
all I feel is spring
as it collects its medals
and passes them on to us.

POPUL VUH

to Octavio Paz

March 14, 1994

Before there was an underworld;
before the forest was populated
with birds and all the things that crawl;
when the trees were naked and bare,
and hiding from the clouds;
the sun created night
as a bed for the moon.

There was a gentle
yellow god who grew vegetables
and tended his soul with flowers.

On the other side of the world
where it rained,
the thunder was the right hand
of a red god
who was fierce,
who wrote laws on stone.

One day the sun met the moon on her way
to visit the stars with some tobacco:
The stars are the
grandmother of the moon.

The sun gazed into the deep black eyes
of the moon and created a man.
From her long silver hair
he created a woman
to hold the hand of the man.

At that,
the sun asked the moon to be his wife.
The moon laughed and her laughter became
the wind and the grass.

The sun wept,
the tears became the almighty waters,

the mistress of thunder and lightning;
and his sadness
wrapped the world in mist and fog.

In anger the sun asked the lady iguana
to dart her tongue into the darkness
for council.
Whereupon the sun gave the man
to the red god,
to be his prince of stone.

He gave the woman
to the yellow god,
so that she would ferment
the rivers with fish.

Each day,
thereafter,
the sun would circle
the waist of the earth
in pursuit of the moon,
who vanished
into religion and blood.

And each day
the sun would light the sky
with shining fruit,
and,
by night,
burn the glowing bed of the moon.

The sun's passion created time and war,
which he scornfully bestowed on the
man and the woman whom he created out
of love for the moon.

The yellow people fought the red people,
until eternity went to sleep,
as the lovers watched the pilgrims of blood
descend to the bottom of the world.

The lovers would die;
their kisses and their words
would become the cities and the cen-
turies,
and their heart beats
the wind.

They were buried in a temple
made of berries and gold;
their feet became
shoots in the earth;
their hands,
the leaves on the trees;
their eyes,
the underground rivers
in the darkness
where lovers meet.

Like all legends,
there is some truth,
when our eyes meet
they become flooded
with the rivers the
lovers have left to us.

THE SPARROW

elegy for Ari Halberstan

March 22, 1994

There was a sparrow
crossing the Brooklyn Bridge.
The sparrow came to us from
heaven to tell us of eternity.

From the desert came a shroud.
It covered the secret of racism
like the dry wind covers fire.
The shroud extinguished
the lamp of heaven
that the sparrow was carrying
and killed the parents of the sparrow.

The dusty shroud knew that
the lamp was the heart of the sparrow
and that long ago when we ate stones
and worshiped sticks,
a drop of blood fell to earth
to become a prayer on Abraham's lips.

The death of a single sparrow
will haunt us
like the making of a child
and God will not come to us
because the air will not be
clean for dreaming.

The sparrows have held
the pieces of the world together
on Saturdays
so that we could sleep late
on Sundays
and drink
on Ash Wednesday.

Moses will remember
the sparrow's face.
The Sabbath will not forgive
the government of meat.
Goliath will chase stones
to redeem his empty soul
because a sparrow will
not return to heaven.

EASTER

to David and Lindsay Shapiro

March 26, 1994

This is Easter:
The season of dead fish
and someone's dried blood
in a cup.

I want to preserve
the secret of the
shriveled leaves
Jesus Christ left
the locust
in his benevolence.

I want to preserve
the tiny clenched fist
of souls tying their
shoes with benedictions
as they drift down
in prayer.

Will I come to rest
in one of God's hands?

The one that holds
Manson and Hitler?

Did the angels ever
visit Auschwitz?

So,
why can't I speak
to God frankly and
discuss the mysteries
of my life?

Each leaf
is a human face
falling to earth.

For a moment
I almost believed
one of them was mine.

PALM SUNDAY

March 27, 1994

Babies are born
in the subways
on Palm Sunday.

They can neither see
nor hear because their
parents are at church
gathering grass for
their collective sins.

Sins are creatures
with academic thoughts.
The Gestapo understood
sin as being intelligent
and misunderstood
and,
perhaps,
even noble.

They protected
their sins
from the blazing sun
and guarded them gently
from the eyes of
ingenuous justice.

They only questioned
the flesh
as sin has no spirit
or soul
to speak of
and would pass them
through the fire
in seconds.

On Palm Sunday
we celebrate
the beginning
and the end of

one Jew
with dead grass,
hand shakes and smiles
to end all the sins
of the world.

THE ORPHAN

March 28, 1994

The mind can harvest
delicate things
and it can also
furrow meaning from words
like love and friendship.

The wind can change an
entire life in the mind
and
significance is afraid
of its own disappearance there.

The mind does not waste
anything it cannot
see or touch
and lives gracefully in a cave
surrounded by thoughts
that connect it to
you and I.

It hordes the past,
the future and the present
but it brightens the past or,
on bright summer days,
the future
because the present
is an orphan
with large black eyes
that listens to a radio
play the same love song
over and over,
again and again.

TATTOO

March 29, 1994

I have a picture of you
tattooed on the palm of my hand.

I keep that hand on my lap
on my way to work in the subway,
and often wonder if anyone
notices that I'm staring at you,
because I remember sleeping
with you in my hand
the night before.

My other hand has an eye
that stares at you
when I take a shower.
The hand with your picture
likes to scratch my head
because you once said
you liked my hair.

When my hand,
the one with the eyes,
answers the phone
when you call,
it blinks
and is overjoyed
to hear your voice
because your picture
cannot talk to it
when I rub both
my hands together.

And if I were to die
without seeing you again,
if I were to die before
I could spend the rest
of my life with you,
the hand with the eye

would lie across my chest
upon my heart
and the one with your picture
would cover my eyes
and both would dream
of you.

PUTA VIDA

April 3, 1994

You're too busy
It's Easter weekend.

Winter is finally over.
The burnt snow will blow away into spring.
The summer air in the city will
glide into your new life.

Perhaps you will even travel on the subways.
Perhaps you will grow a plate of endives
and find my face in it.

You might even watch the ghost
of your old life walk away from you,
despite the hole it has left you.
But you, in fact, will cling to its rim
because your mother is
laughing and watching
everything you do.

You are her comedy of spirits;
a playful thorn she has forgotten
like the tale of your
creation and her pleasure.

THE CEDAR

to Mike and Lynn

April 6, 1994

The shadow of the twentieth century
lives on in my liver with all the dead poets
and artists who drank at the Cedar Bar.

Who said they died for chamber music
and blanquette de veau?
Who said they found one another pounding
glasses of booze against the broken afternoon?

Every night they talked of art and ate museums.
They were the bones of whiskey and the gods of color.
They frightened space with their eyes and apologized to their
brushes because the world could not see them paint.

The critics were stars imitating Rome.
The artists were silent and became New York.

They treated love like relics in a bed
and gave life away for free.
Their hearts bled fresh blood
becoming accidents on white streets
that would hang in museums.

When they spoke about life,
their words became waves of suicide.
Proof that life imitates life.

MY SON

Machu Picchu

April 11, 1994

The mountains love you,
my son,
and they will not fail you.

They will hide you
like my poetry
hides me from you.

The words always hide things.
They are round and hide the sun.

Can a ghost grow up in paradise?
After all,
paradise is made of chamber music.

You have grown up and have a voice.
You will always be my little friendly
ghost who brings me back to life,
because you were created out of water,
snow and music.

ORFEO

to my friends

April 25, 1994

Each hair is a poem I gave my son
Each hair is my allowance from the universe
Each hair is a sunspot on someone's broken heart

The secrets that emerge from the psyche have no floor
They will get off on any floor when you least expect them to
They wear shadows that look like my mother
She could stop God but could not make it snow
She said the weather was a work of art
Like the last streak of wonder
in Medea's heart

You don't have to watch human
Sacrifice on television
Shut your window
Lock the door
Wait for yourself
In the corner
In the night
In the little house
That holds your tears

There is no piano
Just your green velvet
And the years you spent in Russia
As a little box in your mother's womb
With all her curses and her dreams of men

When I write poetry I hear voices:
KennethKoch rubbing his forehead
DavidShapiro swatting words
FrankOHara blowing his noise
PhilipBryant smiling upon me
Neruda drinking red wine
Lorca hailing a cab in New York
Vallejo walking in Paris

RonPadgett calming the world
TedBerrigan dignifying wise-guy poetry
JoeCeravolo on the radio with
Melanoma in the milky sky
Are you asleep?
No
Chopin is asleep on our new sofa
He is wasting his life away
His health looks like a dirty window
His heart has a broken leg
His breathing will go to the grave with him

I'm not the one to part
I'm not the one to hide my feelings
I'm the end of the corridor in your hands
This is a song of war
Because love is music
And its ferocious notes
Are oars that pull us apart

Death is incredible
It is man made
We change the names of the dead
When we bury them
In time they look back at us
And see us
The living
Like old doors in the wind

In the beginning there were small islands
Floating on poetry
These islands belonged to Joe Ceravolo
Joe's words are the body parts of poetry
Like the little children of the fireflies
Who set songs on fire when we cry

There is work to do on top of the forest
There are too many words on top of the forest
They are obstructing our conversation
If the trees aren't pruned our words will never reach

Their destination:
The telephones that hate love
And protect the dead from the living

Will my daughter dress like Venus
Wrapped in exaggerated hopes?
Will the pill invent love for her?
Will her life take place on a
Mental and spiritual planet?
Yes
No
My daughter is a seed full of steam
Leaving me behind like a bad marriage
Helen Helen
My Helen of Troy
Once I placed a kiss on a spider's web
Because there is no evil in nature
The spider laughed
Now the kiss is as free as an insect
And the better part of our love

My other marriages were like the four seasons
That come and go
They have left me small stones
That spend their nights on the balcony of life
Watching Pathos and Comedy celebrate their wedding

Tonight I will write poetry
I will pile the world on my pillow
Like a paramilitary sous chef
Toss an avalanche of flowers
With sunlight and olive oil.

(David Shapiro)

THE PARTICLE POET

Ron Padgett

April 28, 1994

Ron Padgett's hair is a billion years old
An international team of 439 scientists is
Working on his eyes
They have been spinning
In the Fermi National Accelerator
For two decades
The findings were announced today
The Fermilab findings are a major breakthrough
In solving the structural concepts of Modern Poetry
The discovery in all likelihood will never make
A difference to every day poetry in Europe but it
Will give American poets a significant boost
It appears that Ron has validated the standard model
Of New York Poetry central to understanding its meter
Time and Space
The exciting thing is that these are not the only
Pair of eyes that Ron has:
Like all his poems Ron's poems are made of poems
Sometimes they are red poems sometimes they are blue
poems
His theory of poetic excellence for example is the
Epiglottis thin poem that is rather slippery and wet
Very seldom are Ron's poems considered silly
Although sometimes they emulate the auto industry
Some of his longer works should be read at the speed of light
It does help the eructative meter of the work
In rare moments when Ron's poems collide
Between beauty and the world
Our emotions become the rubble of admiration
Heavier than fame
The equivalence of music
That we have lost amid the daily clutter of our lives.

SONATA WITH SOME WATER

Happy Birthday Vincent!

May 1, 1994

I have a goldfish
who is not an evil character
in a black and white newsreel.

My goldfish is in love with my cat.
He calls her on the phone to ask her out.
The cat thinks the fish is Mickey Mouse
with big orange lips.
The goldfish thinks the cat is a fur coat
that sings.

Both the fish and the cat
practice the art of memory.

What is the art of memory?
Scarlet evenings?
Pine trees that think
Smoky The Bear is queer?
Flies that review restaurants
for the *New York Times*?

No.

Memory is the watch your grandfather
gave you before he died.

Ycs.

The one you lost when you were drunk.

Now you are my prisoner:
A voice without a word.
A heart without a wound
to keep the fires burning.

You see,
that is how the world is.
Like my fish and my cat
who pass each other daily

with their opinions of what
they want to see.
The cat is really a position
the goldfish cannot assume.
Nevertheless is nevertheless
to the goldfish.

At night
when the water is tired of both
the goldfish and the family reunion
in the cat's eye, love becomes
a child in a sea
where it is too hot to swim.

FATHER'S DAY

(to Myself)

May 1, 1994

I have seen the seeds in our seeds
Become an army of paper children
The searchlights of pain
Children are brick walls of doubt
Who ask the sky for parents to be the
Primary colors of their lives
Will the children run after
Promises that limp away from them?
An imperfect father gives his
Children a drawing of an old Sun
Water fills the father with tears
And oil like the circus of poetry
The parable of candy is all a
Father can give his children
With its aging lights
Children have no friends
Children are sunspots
Living in their
Parents' erotic snapshots
Kept in a box with
Some half eaten fruit.

ODE TO JULIA CHILD

De re coqinaria

June 1, 1994

When you teach lettuce how to read
You discover the simple chicken liver
The parody of haute cuisine
Where little birds are plucked
From the ceilings of elegant restaurants
And are eaten pink and alive

In a tepidarium consommé
Where Marie Antoinette's head
Is the windshield of history
In every French restaurant
At a table
Where everyone is eating
At a table
Where everyone is sleeping
A henotheism pulverizes clams
To the muffled songs of
Borborygmi!
Borborygmi!

The sorbet is floating in the lake
Like one less pair of eyes
To observe the splendor of the human tongue
One less collection of chemicals
To wonder what it all means
To the clouds of nouvelle cuisine
To the omelet who holds a book
That is bright yellow
Like a thought after lunch

A cream soup is a recurring moment
From another life
Like the thickness of kisses and curry
Love comes from sugar
From green beans

From dawn
Like aromas and sighs
Your colossal wheezing

Is the succusation splash
of the Pièce De Résistance
To the trampoline of faces that enjoy
Goat cheese and fruit
To the woodwinds in the salad
And the vinegar between
Sirius and Antares

Ferculum
Ientaculum
Prandium
Turophile
Gastrique
Au Sec
Maybe

There are women in the artichokes
The thermospodiums of the night
With little butter hearts
Who know clothes have no meaning
After dinner
They whisper things to your organs
They whisper to your natural needs
To the birds that sing in the oven
To the sphinx in your lower colon
To the sirens in your prostate
To you:

perigueux
and your
testicular
black truffles
the synthetic
amulets of love
to your wrinkled
futures
to your little
deaths

Each day a souffle falls like
Samson's hair on a gym floor
Why is a duck born covered with oranges?
Will rosemary and chocolate satisfy
The mouth of the river?
A chef composes a new poem of five star anise
And dedicates it to the skin of an angel
Nirvana is in the marrow
It lies dormant and twisted
Where softly human herbs and gentle water
Rock the syrup in your sleep.

94' PUERTO RICAN DAY PARADE

June 19, 1994

Spring is on the lips of the mannequins
The bars are filled with women
Who are writing the history of bullets
On empty photographs of Puerto Rico
With loud music that tells me I do not exist
I'm the floor of the parade you once walked upon
The warehouse of wishes where you stored
The accessories of my childhood
They are attached to me
Like a small hand following a planet
Like a kiss following you in the dark
Are the police keeping my promises to you?
Are the beggars in the subway offering you my poems?
When my grandmother died
At the center of faith and life
Where she kept the encyclopedia
Of ammonia and anger
My grandfather recited
The story of sex
But she would not stay awake
He was as bright as candy
As he sang to the ice on her lips.

GILLETTE TWIN BLADES

after Philip Bryant

August 25, 1994

The face that falls away from you
Each morning is your face
The lips are biodegradable
as the confessions of zero
So your face is the song of many faces
That play in the winter
Like the colony of faces by the river
Or an evening of faces
With the eyes of a face you once loved
Sometimes the faces one remembers
Are the faces of leaves
Waiting for a woman
With the face of an Arab
Who will beat your heart with stones
Like the face of the lizard that watches
The rainwater swirling past
The end of your life
The faces that conceal the ocean in the night
That remember despair
In the morning
In the mirror
Your razor would rather read the newspaper
Your face is the enemy
The final survivor fatally shot with a smile.

CULO PRIETO

Naranjito/Puerto Rico

September 15, 1994

I do not know what afternoon I will die
I do not know when in the afternoon I will die

The years are not my brother
They have become lullabies of harm
And the fallen trees of my youth

My grandfather told me the palm tree
Was the strongest tree on the island
It could withstand the roof of music
And the pounding shoes of the rain

He told me these things
As he ate running cheese
That hard work was not good for the soul
That the soul needed food and expensive drink
That the end of life was as flat as the world

His life was the introduction to forgiveness
He had the heart of a dam
He was the refill of humor
And to my grandmother
He was the slave of the moon

She was a rare bullet in his heart
That he fondled at night
And like a cloud of decoys
He said to her

> O my tropical infamy
> you are the top of the rain
> hunger is fake happiness without you
> do not die
> I will run for you

YOM KIPPUR

September 15, 1994

Children! Children!
We're having a circumcision festival!
Circumcision and festival are free!
I'm calm
I'm a hero
My father is ashamed
And my mother is the air
That separates life
Each year the months become wolves
Like cactus tears
My son and daughter
Are the sun's microphone
When peace makes friends
With the land mines in the mosques
The song of fire
Prison laughter
And old shirtsleeves
Because
God is not thirsty
Like pain is
It is the public
Who wants tickets to the blame dance
Where atonement
Is a violet prayer
In the book of hands.

MELANGE D'EPICES

September 24, 1994

With milk patties and coriander
The Savage corn flour
Abandons olive oil
To rape the yogurt
Pity the curry and its beaver saffron
When dazed okra is guilty of sassafras
Let us forgive the apple
For not being a pear
Because female truffles raffle thyme
On tree peas and calves' allspice
As fierce as aspic chanting apple lavender
Butter screams wolf basil
With cream of tartar blue
Lighthouse nutmeg
Crustacean fiction
On tribal parsley with lemon grass
And Agamemnon pepper sings the song
Of rabbit salt
To vinegar and melon tears
O happy blessing peas
On vanilla Christmas
With your mocha smiles
Your blueberry illusions
And
Of course
October dessert chocolate.

JOE CERAVOLO

October 19, 1994

Divorce fertilizer
        apache air fare
Are the power of the rock
The young swim for the enemy
And reach the beach of lions
They are all the stars of the woods
Ah felony felony
You are the chocolate of the wolf!
I am the son of lilac
The funnel of corn
Antarctica is the last poet
Not the amputee in the subway
Milk sunsets why is god a harpoon?
May the hand of train bless him
Love is full of noisy names
Coffee shops and soft Pliocene poetry
Like   eros and voiceless sex
Offering   water
        innocent peninsula
Like a   Sunday and jello kisses
Nothing less than summer id
O music Helen
Sleeping dollar bill
Aluminum pleasure
Elevator meat
The yellow hook of Pan
        offering
      the meadow of souls
Yes! Yes!
This is my blood
This is my poem.

MARS

October 20, 1994

"Are you a molecule?"
"No! No!"
"I am Adam."

Atoms have left me for artificial reality
For simulations of human bodies
And their lateral moraines
Because love is faster than the sky
And your breasts are the suns of Andromeda
Where the amperes live in cisterns
Like running water
I'm older than the prairie
An organ with shoulders
That moves from day to day
From one fallen autumn to another
Soon I will be wet like the earth
Full of pain and joy
Like the scars of Mars.

JUDAS ISCARIOT

to the Apostles

November 4, 1994

Christ's words are an oboe
And you are the listeners who must listen
When you sleep with the branches
In the fire
He will go to church to collect your blood
And tear the wings off your sins
They are made of plaster
And covered with dust
The angels around you are keyholes
Where the silence of Christ comes from
You pray to camouflage the decline
Of the messiah
To its hypocritical corpse
To the traditional computer
To the powerless fairy tale
The larvivorous speech of the bible
Is the future tense of your gloom
The sarcophagus contains your fever blisters
And your prayers
Are castanets that laugh
Because you are an adult pin drop
That Christ desires
Like a landscape of new poems
He will collect your spirit
Your last few seconds of joy.

HETERONYM

November 9, 1994

Before gold dreamt of
Jerusalem and Cortez
I warned you of women
The species of double meaning
They are the sleeper's last kiss
Whose name is skin and light
Who are all around us like poetry
Which is difficult enough
It requires old references
Books who talk to themselves
About a boy who created a breast
With no face as round as a poem
I have stolen colors and paper
To cover it with words
I have slept with the breast with no face
I have died everyday for the breast with no face
I am buried alive between the two
I am alive forever between the two
And my mother weeps into the bottom
Of my beloved heteronym
As I lay my childlike face
Against her breast with no face.

RECUERDOS

November 19, 1994

I thought I would never see you again
I'm not the mountain in your life
What business have I with you?

These are the voices of the wondering doctors
They're always muttering in my lungs when I cough your name
I'm as hopeless as a bird telling a lie to the wind

Shall I keep my poems in the freezer for you?
For your children?
For the plumber who secretly reads poetry?

I live in a bundle of unfaithful bones
My heart is a country where you are the president
The feathers in my pillow are your countless
Kisses that follow me to sleep.

REM SLEEP

February 26, 1995

You are the best
Of both worlds
You have tears and teeth
And ask no
Questions
At night
When I sleep
I polish my tail
With imaginary lovers
Because at night
The sky is full with heroes
When the stars are
Running lights
On the ceiling
Walking upside down
Coming toward me with
Their great wings.

BLOOD

March 1, 1995

Those olives
Once lived in Spain
As violet eyes

They belonged to
An African kiss
On my foreskin heart

Water moves history
Deeper into the future
While the uterus churns
Heaven into earth.

HOMENAJE

(Allen Ginsberg/1995)

March 29, 1995

like God
Allen will be taken away from us
to the slaughterhouse of dear God

what will happen to
Allen's great eyes

will he give them to my son
the new poet of life

will Allen become the pieces of the past
the little quiet feast

who will collect
his glasses
who will haunt poetry in Memphis
in the vending machines

we the little children of his soul
are the prostitution tourists
the four dimensional fleas
and our poetry revenant helices

because poets do not sleep
they die like bread

like the id
underneath the tree of secrets
like the dust
underneath the tree of secrets
like the sacred dust of the soul
sounds to a cassette

you are the devastating force
of an old poem
the voice of burning hair
the sarcoma of a minor poet

like me

the idiot in Allen's heart
eating
America tell me poems
writing
kiss me with your round dream poems

WHISPERS

to my son

April 15, 1995

May the whispers and cantatas from heaven join
you in your life like the inches in art

May Kenneth's spirit always dwell in your green
syntax

May the well of David's poetry touch your writing
hand

May the anomalous spirit of Mozart keep a glove in
your heart

May the blue beaches of music always embrace you
when you arrive with your poetic snowman

May you always be a flying star pushing the beginning
of creation to the open door

May the memory of birds swim blindly in your
heart like astronauts in cold outer space

May the conquistador's ivory blood and the roses
in Montezuma's skull stitch your life together

And may the crayon hands and snakes swim with me
and my father who is a cave full of gifts from you.

OKLAHOMA AMERICA

April 25, 1995

The fathers of America
have ruined the mountains
The mothers of America
have dried the river beds
The children of America
are dying at play
Our forefathers watch our
neonates mouse the words of freedom
Worms vagrant fallopian worms

Are birds freedom?
Are children sheep?

This is the year of the bullet
Of white professional homework
Of Nagasaki fertilizer
Of cheap fuel oil
Of tender SS movies
This is oncotic Americana
This is why fish will fly to heaven

We are the widow of our dreams
We are shrinking in their skin
We are attached to their wisdom

Look at the thermos colored sky
Fame flying on TV
They wash their hands in our womb
Where the dead know the stars
Are sleeping children
Like the procession of the equinox
Condensing our fate

We are the Furies of entropy
We have killed
A hundred sixty million
Human trees this century

Who will wear their clothes?
Death is as round as an apple
Holding a child ever so gently

They no longer see the kangaroo
They cannot touch
The innocent mirror
With their wet hands
The tears are drowning
In their sand pails
Like lyrical lips
The mothers will never be
The sun on their faces

O my beloved country
Where is the antelope of love?
Why does the earth
Turn away from the sun?
Why are the children covered
With concrete
Rain
And neglected
Specks of freedom?

HIJA

Christophe

June 4, 1995

Is a sleeping doll in paradise
Her thoughts are small plates
That fly to the moon

Her face is the axis of my life
Where the desert ends

When she arrives I become
A bell full of water

With her look from her mother's eyes
The little ice cubes in God's hand

That He gave to the blue sky
And the underwater fish

What is the telephone without
A daughter?

A thump
Without a bug to squash.

June 23, 1995

The car god
smiles
at the little
holes it has
left
in the wind

BREAD & WATER

June 30, 1995

What good am I if I'm not a fish?
A loaf of bread?
Are my lips made of bullets?
The day has lost its faucet
Its grip on life

I rinse my mouth with your daily morning
Because you are the spatula
Used to create windows
The clouds in the hospitals
On your submarine white skin
Like lungs dreaming of veiny gas
Against the drops of night

Ignition
Is where aeriferous shame
Falls on noisy streets
Incomplete without your hideouts
Your softness has a thousand legs

There was sleep before life
Strangers came with cars before God
With their maps of Eskimos
And their tombs of passion
From the whale's room

Women are rivers that water children
They are the ropes of their fathers
Like the passion in the desert
They die in their father's hands
They are the ants of Israel

Is it only souls that can become bees?
There are trillions of them without wings
Like rags between your mother's prayers

Beloved balm of her placenta
The whisper of cakes to me
Ancient wife to all my fingers

My Venus fleeting seconds
You are my daily loss
I am the kiss banging at your door
You are keys I have lost.

"THE BLOOD OF THE CHIEFTAINS RAN LIKE WATER"

Juan de Alvarado's, "Tonatio", "the Sun",
massacre at the feast of Toxcatl, Tenochtitlan
Florentine Codex, Book xii

July 30, 1995

Moctezoma is drowning
In his own sacred blood
He whispers to Cortés
Who is not there

where is Hannibal?
why doesn't Dante speak to me?
you promised
for excavating my body

Which no longer exists
Only your allergy to gold

Cortés Cortés

You leave me
The resonance of steel
From your luminous hand
The short marriage of life
The inescapable kiss of death
Like a pale pink sky
On ornamental corn
Like quiet scallop shells
Folding each other up
Breathing a little smoke
Into the heart
That coughs
Giving life to the sun

Cortés Cortés

Will my avocado trees pledge
Fealty to the king of snow in
Spain?

Will my daughters faint when
They see the naked blood of
Christ?

Why do you want to make our children
Pink rubella
Like the sonic rage in Alvarado's
Eyes?

While their little fists clutch the
Canal in the sky in their mother's
Breasts
My bones will turn into the dust of
Flowers
Your bones into the dust of
Fever

Your gold will fly like bees
Across the wet grasses of the sea
With the gliding centuries over our graves

Your god is a giant skewer
Looking for mosquitoes who wait a lifetime
For a pious hand to crush them

Cortés Cortés

I die alone without you
Without my own sacred blood
With the heart of a dog that
Licks your white hand

"You have ruined yourselves and me also"

Because studying time and murder
Is the soul of man
The spiteful silence of a dream

Cortés Cortés

“as a song
I was born
as a flower
I will
die...”

THE ANGELS

July 31, 1995

The angels have appointed
A dog to hide our secrets
The ones we touch
The ones we keep
The ones that live in a room
That become part of lives
Like the lichens on the moon
Secrets are the game of God
He likes ice cream cake
And soda
And house wives
That look unhappy
Attending early mass
Because there is beer in heaven
And don't forget the big blue church
With the piano bar in the sky
Across the street
Where the angels meet
With the dog
Who shares our secrets.

IT'S OVER

August, 1995

death is a lover
full of memories

when things are over
it comes to us

with little

toy cars and pink hands
it knows we are twisted with love

like a hotel of smiling whores
it knows we are the effigies of the womb

THE MASHGIACH

David & Daniel Shapiro

September 25, 1995

All the same God is a dream
Who listens to trapped stones
And blades of grass
This is why we are shadows
In God's eyes
Pursuing the sweet worms
Imagining them to be flowers
Who thinks of having a wife
More strongly then God?
Or as a stone more precious
To Him than pain?
He even loves her shadow
That catches fire when He sleeps.

LOVE

January 18, 1996

My tired bones only think of you
some are faithful to me when I think of you

like friends on a high school summer day
like the islands in your eyes

let me sleep among your fine feathers
with the tiny stones in your long gracious hands

that touch the world when it sheds its leaves
when love is a ribbon around oblivion

waiting for the sea to come to school
dressed in white and salt

the kisses I send you are little
patches of fog that bark at the sea.

SPOT

January 20, 1996

Like I said
The spot on your nose is magical

I've known that spot since I was a boy
I think we should pass it on to our children

I love the laughter of your spot
I live for that spot

There is nothing in the world like your spot
I keep asking your petit four nose

Is it from a peach tree?
Is it the fur from your mother and father's kisses?

I want to be the paw that sleeps on the spot when
It becomes the heart of our slumbering children

HELEN VALENTINE

February 14, 1996

I want to bury the morning
and erase the coffee from

The nights of the world
tumbling down the hillside of sleep

below the relentless stars
The days and weeks are piling up

as I go on stuffing myself with memories
on my way to work in my uncomfortable shoes.

RELIQUIAE

May, 1996

The universe is shrinking
Like a small lifeboat
The great chunks
Will never fit again
They are as innocent
As   Casal's Bach
        Whispers eating
The sound out of the air
      Replicas
Of handmade
         Breasts
Made in Mexico
Of saffron and chocolate
On the lips of Puerto Rico
The sun ends its life
With a wet kiss

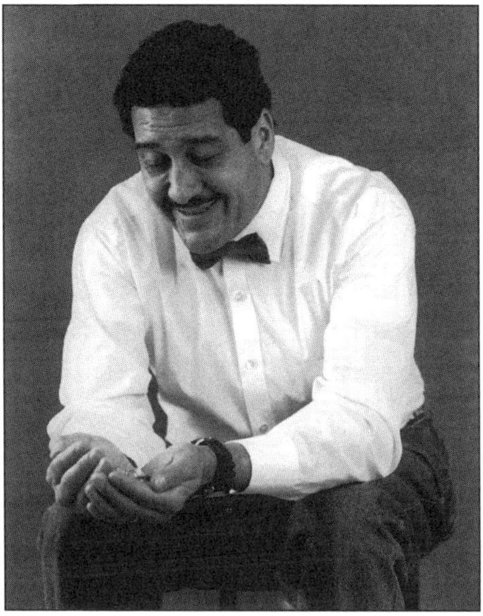

Frank Lima was born in New York City in Spanish Harlem, 1939. His parents were Mexican and Puerto Rican. He received a Master's from Columbia University in 1975. During the '60s and '70s he published three books of poetry *(Inventory*, Tibor de Nagy Gallery, 1964; *Underground with the Oriole*, E.P. Dutton, 1971; *Angel*, W.W. Norton, 1976) and was included in numerous anthologies. In the late '70s Lima dropped out of the poetry world (although he would continue to write) to devote his time to his family and pursue a career in the culinary arts. Trained in his youth, in classical French cooking, he is now a teacher at the New York Restaurant School.

Profile Series

The Desires of Mothers to Please Others in Letters
Bernadette Mayer

Heart of the Breath (Poems 1979-1992)
Jim Brodey

Burnt House to Paw Paw: Appalachian Notes
Merrill Gilfillan

Inventory: New & Selected Poems
Frank Lima

Series Editor: Michael Gizzi